BASIC SCENERY
for Model Railroaders
— SECOND EDITION —

Lou Sassi

KALMBACH BOOKS

Kalmbach Books
21027 Crossroads Circle
Waukesha, Wisconsin 53186
www.Kalmbach.com/Books

Published in 2014
18 17 16 15 14   1 2 3 4 5

Manufactured in the United States of America

ISBN: 978-0-89024-946-8
E-ISBN: 978-1-89024-947-5

Editor: Jeff Wilson
Art Director: Tom Ford
Designer: Lil Weber

Unless otherwise noted, all photographs were taken by the author.

Library of Congress Cataloging-In-Publication Data
Sassi, Lou.
   Basic scenery for model railroaders / Lou Sassi. -- Second edition.

   pages : color illustrations ; cm. -- (Model railroader books) -- (Essentials series)

   Issued also as an ebook.
   ISBN: 978-0-89024-946-8

   1. Railroads--Models--Design and construction--Handbooks, manuals, etc. 2. Models
and modelmaking--Handbooks, manuals, etc. I. Title. II. Series: Model railroader books.

TF197 .S267 2014
625.1/9

Contents

Introduction

A Rutland Alco rolls a few freight cars along a street next to the Peerless tanning company. The ground cover, power lines and poles, signs, street surface, and other scenic details all add to the realism of this HO scale scene.

I was introduced to scale model railroading on a chilly day in December 1958. It was noon hour, and I was on a break from classes at Saratoga Springs High School, where I was a freshman. As I surveyed the shelves of the local newsstand for something to read, I caught a glimpse of a magazine called *Model Railroader*.

Picking up the magazine and leafing through the pages, I came across a layout story about the HO scale Texas & Rio Grande Western Railroad written by Bill McClanahan. A few pages later I found a section called "Trackside Photos." I was particularly impressed by the photos of a Shay steam locomotive crossing a spindly trestle (built by Cliff Grandt) and a three-quarter view of a steam locomotive spotted at a freight house (built by Jack Work). I was amazed at how the detailed structures and scenery brought the model trains to life.

Regardless of scale, scenery doesn't have to be complex to be effective.

Fast-forward to 1982. After years of experimenting with plaster, sawdust, and all sorts of concoctions in pursuit of the creation of my miniature hills and dales, I happened upon a book, *How to Build Realistic Model Railroad Scenery*, written by Dave Frary and edited by Bob Hayden. I was again amazed. Here were two guys who actually went out into the woods and fields by their homes and found the raw materials of "real" scenery with which to make model scenery. They used lichen for trees and dirt to make DIRT! All this stuff was affixed to the layout using white glue and water.

It was very fortunate that Dave and Bob chose to write their book when they did because it corresponded to the time I started construction of my HO scale Boston & Maine West Hoosic Division. Since then, my scenery techniques have been influenced and altered by a number of other people. One in particular, a fellow named Ken Olsen, decided to share his ideas about scenery at a number of National Model Railroad Association national conventions. I was sure to be in the front row at every one of them. Among other things, he introduced me to such ideas as furnace-filter-and-sphagnum-moss evergreen trees, peppergrass hardwoods, and most important, a concoction I call "ground goop."

After a number of years experimenting with the ideas and techniques I had learned from these and other folks, I was contacted by fellow modeler Bob Hamm. Bob had met two fellows at a local round-robin train group that were experimenting

with their own scenery techniques. Knowing my interest in the subject, Bob thought it might be fun if the four of us got together and started sharing our ideas. I agreed, and the resulting "Tree Group" became one of the most enjoyable, informative groups I had ever been involved with. Some of the fruits of those Wednesday night meetings were shared with our fellow modelers in the May, July, September, and November 1995 issues of *Model Railroader* magazine.

In 2009 my wife, Cheryl, and I decided it was time to leave the Northeast and its endless winters for a warmer climate. Knowing that my old HO layout would not be making the trip, I decided that it was time for an entirely new approach to scale (On30 this time) and scenery making. I wanted something that would be light and portable. Extruded foam seemed to be the answer and as you will see in the chapters that follow I believe it was! Also, because of my switch in scales you will find scenes in both HO and O scale in this book. I have learned one very important thing since switching scales. Scenery materials and techniques used in HO scale can, in most cases, easily be adapted to work in O and other scales.

Einstein I'm not

As you may have surmised by now, the projects that follow are a collection of techniques I have learned over the years. I will be the first to admit that I am not ingenious enough to

have invented them all myself. Many have been culled from the work of others. You can look at this book as a conglomeration of some of my own ideas along with those of others that I have used in their original form or altered to suit my needs.

Many of these techniques were used to prepare the West Hoosic Division for its appearances in Allen Keller's *Great Model Railroads* video series (no. 23) and Kalmbach's annual *Great Model Railroads* magazine (1999). I believe all of them are worthy of your consideration as a viable means to an end—that end being realistic miniature scenery.

There is one particularly important observation that you must bear in mind if your miniature scenery is going to look believable. After studying the woods and fields in my area first-hand, I have noticed that foliage—be it grass, bushes, or trees—has a constant base hue that ties everything together, regardless of variations in color, and it is not that difficult to replicate. Just like Mother Nature, we have to make our colors blend. This blending of colors will take place as you follow the projects in this book. Although the products used for each project range from natural to manmade (many by different manufacturers), I have made sure they are color-compatible.

Enough philosophy. Let's get to work . . . or play, if you wish. I hope you enjoy tackling this series of projects as much as I've enjoyed preparing them for you. Happy model railroading!

CHAPTER ONE

Foam base for scenery and track

The wind came up while the boys were unloading the Baltimore & Ohio car and blew the Styrofoam panels away. Bob Seckler throws his arms up in frustration. The HO scale scene features Rutland RS-3 No. 405.

Even though you can't see it, the base that lies beneath the visible scenery is as important as the vegetation and details that draw viewers' attention. This chapter highlights the initial steps in the construction of a 2 x 6-foot HO scale diorama which will feature a small farm complex, urban roadway, and a large mill, pond, waterfall, and cascading stream. You can follow the same guidelines on a module or permanent layout in any scale.

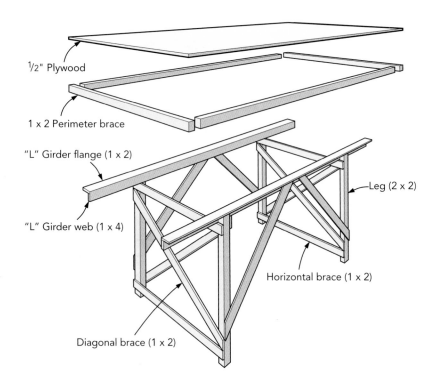

½" Plywood

1 x 2 Perimeter brace

"L" Girder flange (1 x 2)

"L" Girder web (1 x 4)

Leg (2 x 2)

Horizontal brace (1 x 2)

Diagonal brace (1 x 2)

Materials:

Woodland Scenics:
- Assorted thickness foam sheets, risers, and inclines
- Foam Putty
- Foam Tack Glue
- Foam Nails
- Low-Temp Glue Sticks

Miscellaneous:
- Homabed or other roadbed
- Masking tape
- No. 6 x ¾" flathead wood screws
- (1) 4 x 8-foot sheet of tempered Masonite

Although this isn't a book about benchwork, it's important to understand that scenery design begins with your benchwork base. For this project, I decided to try Woodland Scenics' Subterrain System methods and materials. The entire scene is built on a solid base of ½"-thick plywood.

After years of building layout framework out of saber-saw-cut plywood supported by risers and frame members made from dimensional lumber (1 x 2s and 1 x 4s), I longed for an alternative that was easier to work with

and lighter in weight. In the past I had used blue and pink extruded Styrofoam (the kind used for home insulation) as a scenery base, but I continued to use the old tried-and-true laminate of either ½" Homabed or Homasote glued to ½" plywood as a roadbed.

I have been using Homabed as a track base for years. Homabed is cut from Homasote—a pressed-fiber board sold as wall insulation. Homabed has been on the model railroad market for years. It is precut in solid and notched 3-foot lengths with beveled

sides that create a realistic ballast slope. Homasote is made by California Roadbed Company. (See the Appendix on page 94 for all manufacturers' contact information.)

One day I discovered the Woodland Scenics Subterrain System. This consists of 1½-pound density foam risers, inclines, and profile boards of various thicknesses. I found foam sheets and the Woodland Scenics system handy, but the one thing I didn't like about working with foam was the tools for cutting and shaping it. The popular choices were a Stanley Surform rasp/file or hot wire foam cutter. The file creates thousands of electrostatically charged particles that stuck to everything and anything within a hundred yards of the project. The hot wire cutter is cleaner to work with, but takes too long to do the job and is limited in the thickness and depth of material it could cut.

Woodland Scenics has since come to the rescue with another tool for cutting foam panels: the Hot Knife (no. ST1438), which makes cutting

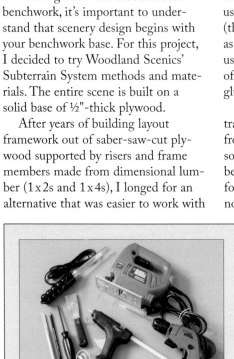

Tools:

Woodland Scenics:
- Foam Knife and Foam Hot Knife
- Foam Pencil
- Low-Temp Foam Glue Gun

Miscellaneous:
- Putty knife
- Ruler
- NMRA track gauge
- Saber saw
- Phillips screwdriver

1

Mark the track center line with a foam pencil or other marker. Remove the track, then connect the dots to make a continuous track line.

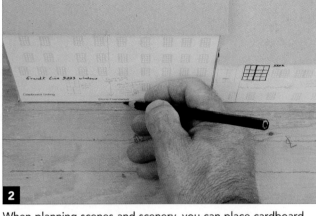

2

When planning scenes and scenery, you can place cardboard mockups of structures (or the actual buildings) to test their visual impact and determine their final locations.

3

Hot-glue the risers in place. Make sure the risers are centered on the drawn track center line.

4

Make the siding ⅛" lower than the main line. This helps make it look more like the real thing, where siding tracks typically have a lower profile than the main.

the foam a much cleaner and easier process. I now use the Hot Knife for all major cutting while resorting to the Surform tool for fine-tuning the foam.

I also picked up a good tip from good friend and fellow modeler Bob Lawson, a Cincinnati-area modeler who was in the process of building his own layout. Bob used sheets of white 1½-pound-density foam in varying thicknesses as a scenery base, instead of the more common 2-pound density (blue and pink) foam. Whereas the Woodland Scenics panels are 18 x 24 inches and range in thickness from ¼" to 4", the panels that Bob uses are 2 x 4 feet and 1" to 6" thick.

Bob obtains his white foam panels from a drywall supply house in the Cincinnati area. Check building supply stores (especially those catering to contractors) in your area for a source. I now use these larger, thicker panels

to form the base for the landscape and track, with the thinner/smaller Woodland Scenices panels for fine tuning the final elevations, track, and road undulations.

Keep in mind that when cutting foam with a hot wire tool or foam knife, you are creating toxic fumes. The tool is actually melting the foam and in doing so is releasing polycyclic aromatic fumes that contain hydrocarbons, carbon soot, and carbon monoxide. Because of this, cut foam in a well ventilated area. It's also a good idea to wear a respirator-style facemask for protection.

Construction

For my first effort I built a 2½ x 6-foot-base of ½" plywood framed with 1 x 2 lumber around its perimeter. To this frame I will later attach the fascia, made with ½" tempered Masonite

hardboard. This all sits on two 1 x 4 L-girders which, in turn, were supported by two sets of 2 x 2 legs. The drawing on page 7 shows the details.

I drew the center line of my track-work in pencil directly onto the plywood, **1**. I used cardboard mockups of structures to test for size, track clearance, and visual impact, **2**.

Once I was satisfied with the location of everything, I hot-glued the Woodland Scenics foam track risers in place on the plywood. Since I wanted an 8" vertical drop from track level to the lowest ground level (the bottom of the waterfall and a cascading stream), I stacked two 4" risers on top of one another and hot-glued them together, **3**.

I wanted the siding at Peerless to be at a slightly lower grade than the main line, so I used a thinner riser and added a piece of ¼" sheet stock to make the

Hot-glue the mill pond base—a 4"-thick piece of foam—into position. Smaller blocks of 4" foam elevate the base to the proper height.

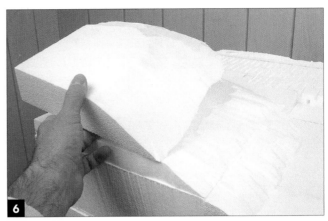

Build up the hillside around the pond with various thicknesses of foam sheet. I contoured the pieces with the Woodland Scenics Hot Knife and Hot Wire Cutter.

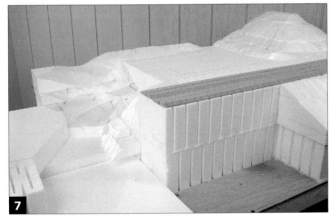

Temporarily place all of the smaller foam pieces that make up the waterfall. When you're satisfied with the results, glue them in position.

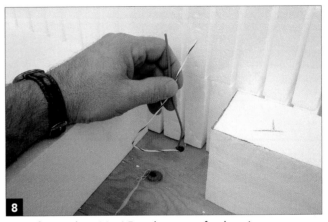

Don't forget the wiring! Run the power feeder wires up through the plywood base, making sure they're long enough to reach the track.

elevation of the siding ⅛" lower than the main line, 4. Once the risers for the track were in place I started stacking sheet stock foam up to track level. Rather than use solid sheets all the way up to track level I cut blocks of 4" sheets and attached full sheets to the tops of them.

In photo 5, you can see the base for the mill pond being placed on top of 4" blocks that were, in turn, hot glued to the plywood base. I made a sloping hillside beside the mill pond by stacking sheets of Styrofoam of varying thicknesses on top of one another, 6, and shaping them to a hilly contour.

At this stage of construction you must decide what you are going to use for "water" in the pond and streambed. If you use Enviro-Tex, as I did, you must protect the surface of the foam. Enviro-Tex is a two-part clear polymer that, when mixed, can be poured in

place. When it cures, it dries to a hard, high-gloss sheen.

If you don't protect the surface, the Enviro-Tex will eat through the foam and you will have a miniature open-pit mine instead of a pond. You can seal the pond base, sides, and stream bed with a couple layers of plaster cloth, but scenery master Dave Frary recommends that, in order to prevent the "water" from eventually discoloring, it's best to cut a piece of ⅛" thick Masonite hardboard to fit between the foam and the Enviro-Tex. The Masonite must fit under the final layers of foam that form the perimeter of the pond, so don't attach them permanently at this time.

With the pond base and hillside finished, I turned my attention to the dam and cascading waterfall. I developed this area by cutting and fitting various shapes and thicknesses

of foam together to create a series of three falls that would carry the water from the dam, around a curve, beneath the track, and off the layout. I used foam nails to hold everything in place until I had test-fit the entire area, 7. Once this was done, I built up the foam on the opposite side of the stream to form a base for the farm scene. Before adding the finished solid foam panels opposite the mill and farm, I installed track feeder wires by first drilling a ½" hole through the plywood base, then feeding the wires through it, 8, and tying them off, leaving enough excess wire so I could solder it to the rails later.

With all the foam in place it was time to fill any voids in the material and add the roadbed. Since I planned to attach the Homabed directly to the risers and not cover them with plaster gauze, as Woodland Scenics suggests,

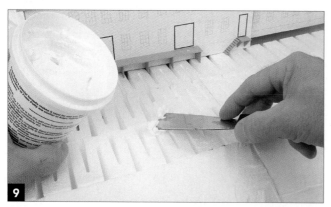

Fill voids in the foam risers with Woodland Scenics Foam Putty. A small spatula works well and makes the job go quickly.

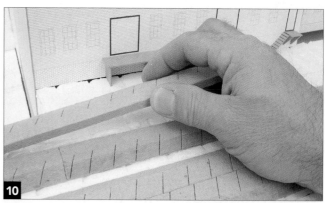

Glue the Homabed roadbed (or your roadbed material of choice) in place atop the risers. Use pins (Woodland Scenics calls them "Foam Nails") to hold it in place until the glue dries.

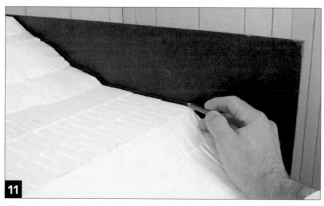

Clamp or tack the hardboard fascia panels in place, then use the scenery contour as a guide for marking the inside edge of the fascia for cutting.

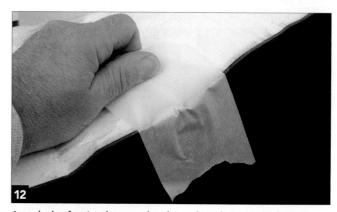

Attach the fascia, then apply white glue along top edge of foam. Tape the fascia to the foam until the glue dries.

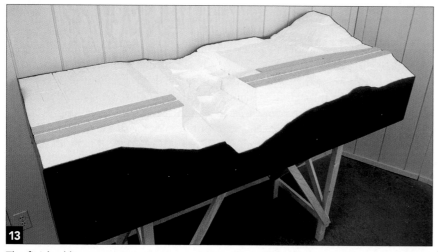

The finished layout section awaits scenicking. Regardless of the benchwork, roadbed, and track methods and products you use, it's the overall layout contour that matters most in providing a good base for scenery cover and texture.

I filled the gaps in the risers with (Woodland Scenics) Foam Putty. This looks like spackling compound but is lighter weight and less dense. It applies easily with a putty knife, **9**. Once the putty dried, I applied full-strength white glue to the back of the Homabed and pressed it in place, **10**, using Foam Nails to hold it until the glue dried.

One tip: I always use Elmer's white glue for these and other scenery projects. I've tried white glue from other manufacturers and had mixed results. Avoid products called "school glue" (from Elmer's and others), as it looks like white glue but behaves differently when mixed with water.

I chose ⅛" tempered Masonite hardboard for the side fascia panels. After carefully measuring the length of each side of the module, I cut four panels from a 4x8-foot sheet. I temporarily attached each panel to the module with no. 6 wood screws into the 1x2 strips that I had previously attached to the bottom of the plywood base. I marked the ground (foam) contours along the top edge of each panel with a foam marking pencil, **11**, then removed the panels and cut along the contour lines with a saber saw. I applied white glue to the top edge of the foam sheets and temporarily taped the Masonite to the foam until the glue dried, **12**.

Photo **13** shows the layout awaiting final scenicking.

CHAPTER TWO

Modular frame with a foam base

In Chapter 1, I showed how to build foam scenery and a track base on a sheet of ½" plywood. This time we are going to eliminate the plywood. By doing so we will make things lighter in weight and therefore more portable—a valuable asset for modules and sectional layouts.

Dana Aldrich and Ed West unload a shipment of Styrofoam. This book shows you how to build this On2½ scene.

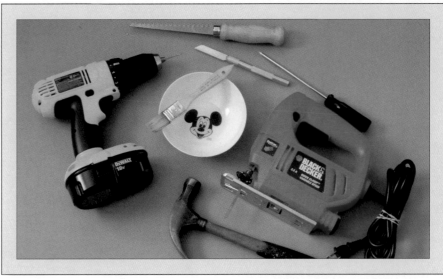

Tools:

Woodland Scenics:
- Modular Benchwork (2 modules)
- Foam Knife and spare blades
- Foam Pencils
- Low-Temp Foam Glue Gun
- Hot-Wire Foam Cutter

Miscellaneous:
- Hot Knife (Demand Products)
- Putty knife, brushes
- Ruler
- NMRA track gauge
- Saber saw, cordless drill

I started construction on my HO scale West Hoosic Division railroad in 1978. For 30 years it provided me with enjoyment. I must confess, however, that in 1964, years before starting the WHD, I read Lynn Moody's book, *The Maine Two Footers*. This experience left me yearning to try my hand at re-creating, in miniature at least, a portion of the largest of the Maine slim-gauge railroads, the Sandy River & Rangeley Lakes.

Unfortunately, in the 1960s there were not many models available, in any scale, of Maine two-foot gauge equipment. However, in 2006, while working on *How to Build and Detail Model Railroad Scenes, Volume 2*, I came upon a 2-4-4T Forney locomotive in On30 by Bachmann which reignited my interest in the Maine two footers. About this time my wife, Cheryl, and I were discussing a possible move south, away from the endless winters of upstate New York. After a bit of consternation and discussion we decided that it was time to not only change our living location but also my model railroad's scale and prototype. This time, however, I did not want to build myself into a corner, so to speak, with my layout construction techniques. I had built the West Hoosic using Linn Westcott's L-girder benchwork with a ½" plywood-½" Homasote laminate for a track base. While undeniably strong, this approach to benchwork construction did not lend itself to portability.

With this in mind, I decided to make an O scale diorama of Strong on the Sandy River the subject of several book chapters.

The plan was simple: I would build the town as a layout section—essentially a 2x6-foot diorama—making it as portable as possible. That

Materials List:

Woodland Scenics:
- Assorted thickness foam sheets
- Assorted thickness foam risers
- Assorted thickness foam inclines
- Foam Putty
- Foam Nails
- Low-Temp Glue Sticks

Miscellaneous:
- Homabed roadbed
- Masking tape
- No. 8 x 2", 2½" drywall screws
- 4 x 8-foot sheet of tempered Masonite hardboard

way, once the book was finished, the module could be easily transported so I could bring it south when we moved. The module would then become the basis for a new model railroad.

I started planning the Strong scene for portability. Traditional L-girder construction was out. I decided instead to use two Woodland Scenics pre-fab modules, **1**. Each of these is 18" wide and 3 feet long and consists of a 1x4 pressboard frame mounted on four 2x2 pine legs. All components are predrilled and include all the hardware necessary for assembly, including four sets of T-nuts and elevator bolts to finely adjust the leg length/layout height.

On top of these modules I planned to glue a double layer of extruded foam as a scenery base with Homabed (a commercial roadbed material made from Homasote insulation board) glued directly to the Styrofoam as a track base. There would be no L-girders, no risers, and no ½" plywood to add weight.

When I later dismantled the West Hoosic layout, I ended up with many linear feet of 1x2 pine boards. Because of this, I decided that when construction of the new layout started I would build my own sections using this wood rather than using more modules from Woodland Scenics. This would also allow me to alter the length and width of each section to my liking. If you go this route, you can buy all of the hardware locally—I got mine from

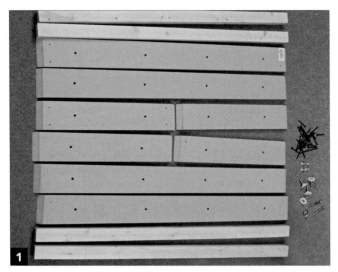

Here's what you get with Woodland Scenics module kits. The parts are pre-cut and holes are drilled out.

Attach the framework parts with drywall screws. A cordless drill makes quick work of the process.

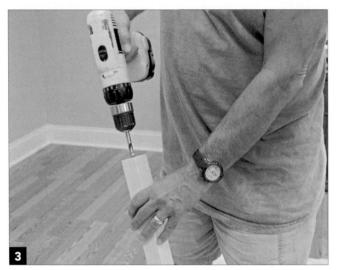

Drill a mounting hole in the bottom of each leg to accept a T-nut. This makes it easy to level the layout.

Use a hammer to lightly tap each T-nut into place.

Secure the sections together with lag bolts. You can use standard nuts, but wing nuts make it easy to later separate the sections if needed.

Screw the shelving in place, again using drywall screws. Two screws in each end of each board is sufficient.

7

Here's the completed shelving on the lowest level. The boards are notched in the corners to clear the legs.

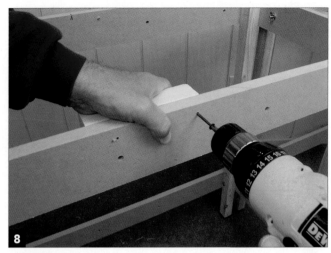

8

Mount several short horizontal 2x2 brace supports along the inside top edges of the framework.

9

Screw the 2x2 horizontal braces into position from above.

10

Attach vertical fascia supports (9"-long 2x2s) to the ends of the horizontal braces.

my local Lowe's home improvement store. As with the Woodland Scenics modules, I used 2"- to 2½"-long no. 8 drywall screws to assemble each of my own sections, **2**. I also drilled holes, **3**, and added T-nuts for elevator bolts to the bottom of the legs, **4**.

Once each module was assembled and in position I bolted them together with ¼" x 20 x 2" hex bolts and wing nuts, **5**. To aid in storage, before adding decking to the modules, I added shelves to hold plastic storage containers. This consisted of 1 x 4s mounted on top of 1 x 2s that were in turn mounted to the sides of the lower cross members of the framework, **6, 7**.

Since I wanted the surface of the layout to be 2 to 3 feet wide, rather than the 18" of the modules, I screwed lengths of 2 x 2s to the sides of the

1 x 4 framework, **8**, and mounted 2- or 3-foot-long 2 x 2 horizontal cross members to them, **9**. These would support the Styrofoam. Next I attached 9"-long 2 x 2s vertically to the horizontal cross members, **10**. These will eventually support a ⅛" hardboard fascia.

I notched the blue Styrofoam panels with a hole saw, applied full-strength Elmer's white glue to the tops of the horizontal 2 x 2s, **11**, and set the panels into position, **12**. I placed various objects onto the Styrofoam to hold it down while the glue dried, **13**.

The lower (blue) layer of foam is 2" thick extruded board. This is 2-pound density foam and is available at home-improvement stores in 2 x 8 or 4 x 8-foot sheets, and can also be pink depending on manufacturer. The top layer of foam is 2" thick white

board. It's not as rigid (1½ lb. density, the same as Woodland Scenics' foam panels) as the blue or pink board, and therefore it will flex easier.

Once the white glue holding the bottom panels in place dried, I removed the weights, cut the white upper panels to fit, spread full strength Elmer's white glue over the bottom panels with a brush, and set the upper panels in place, **14**. Again I sat weights on the panels until the glue dried.

Once the weights were removed I applied white glue to the bottom of the Homabed roadbed, **15**, placed the Homabed directly onto the upper layer of Styrofoam, and pinned it in place with Woodland Scenics foam nails until the glue dried, **16**. Once the track is added, we're ready to begin adding scenery.

Use a small brush to apply a thin coat of white glue to the tops of the 2x2 horizontal braces.

Place the blue foam into position. Cut the notches and test-fit the piece *before* adding the glue.

Add weights (almost anything will work) on top of the foam panels until the glue dries.

Use a wide brush to spread white glue over the entire blue foam board and place the white foam panels into position.

Add your choice of roadbed as needed. I chose Homabed, a pressed fiber material made from Homasote, which is commonly used as insulation. Spread white glue on the contact surface.

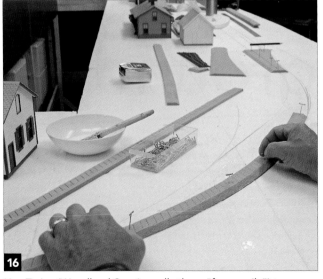

Use T-pins (Woodland Scenics calls them "foam nails") to hold the roadbed in place until the glue dries. Make sure the roadbed is pressed firmly to the surface.

CHAPTER THREE

Adding basic ground cover

Southern 4-6-0 No. 909 passes Peerless Tanning Company in an HO scene. Getting a simple layer of ground cover on a layout is a major factor in creating a realistic scene. Compare this to how the area looked unfinished (see Chapter 1, page 10, photo 13).

Because of America's agricultural heritage, much of our rural countryside consists of cleared but uncultivated farm fields. Using a combination of natural and commercial materials, it is quite simple to replicate these open fields in miniature. Just bear in mind that, as always, a variety of texture and color is the secret to believable scenery.

Tools:

- Fine-, medium-, and coarse-mesh kitchen sieves
- Magnet
- Small paintbrush
- Artist's spatula
- Spoon
- Eyedroppers
- Spray bottle
- Rave Mega Hold hairspray

The primary natural material for an open field is plain old dirt, which is economical and widely available from nature. Medium to dark browns and grays work the best. Stay away from anything containing clay, as mixing a clay-based soil with water will result in a slimy mess. You also don't want to use anything with magnetic particles in it. Passing a magnet over your dirt will help determine if this is a problem. I sift the dirt through a number of progressively finer mesh kitchen sieves and categorize the results in Tupperware containers. This way I can better control the texture of the material during application.

Other natural materials I like to use are ground-up leaves and pine needles. I grind these in a food blender then run them through the same kitchen sieves as the dirt. See Chapter 7 for details on prepping these materials.

When it comes to commercial products, I use an assortment of ground foams and polyfiber mesh to represent grass and weeds. My favorite open-field ground foams are AMSI (Agricultural Model Supply Inc.) spring green, yellow green, and grass green. I also use Woodland Scenics green blended turf. For higher brush I sprinkle the finer foams over Woodland Scenics polyfiber mesh and pieces of buffing pad left over from my conifer tree projects (see the next

Materials:

AMSI:
- Spring green foam (fine), 401
- Spring green foam (coarse), 402
- Yellow green foam (fine), 411
- Yellow green foam (coarse), 412
- Grass green foam (fine), 441
- Grass green foam (coarse), 442
- Ground cover material, 30001G
- Ground cover material, 30002G

Woodland Scenics:
- Blended turf foam, 49
- Polyfiber mesh, 178

Miscellaneous:
- Vermiculite
- Celluclay (Activa Products)
- Elmer's Glue-All (white glue)
- Lysol disinfectant (concentrate)
- Earth-brown paint such as Pittsburgh Tobacco Brown interior flat latex, 7607
- Nonmagnetic dirt
- Tea leaves

Sort dirt by sifting it through progressively finer kitchen sieves. Store the materials in plastic containers based on color and texture.

From right to left are ground-up pine needles, ground-up leaves, and ground-up leaves that have been run through a fine kitchen sieve.

The components of "ground goop" include white glue, paper mache, earth-color latex paint, Lysol, and Vermiculite.

chapter). These materials are fixed in place with hairspray.

I use a concoction called "ground goop" as a base for all my ground textures. You'll find ground goop used in several chapters and projects throughout this book. Ground goop is a mix of 1 cup Celluclay, 1 cup Vermiculite, 1 cup earth-colored latex paint (I use Pittsburgh no. 7607 Tobacco Brown), ⅔ cup white glue, and one capful of Lysol (concentrate) or similar disinfectant. The Lysol prevents mold buildup when the material is in storage. Add enough tap water to this concoction to bring it to the consistency of natural peanut butter.

Begin by brush-painting whatever base material you are using with earth-color paint before applying the ground goop. This prevents any raw plaster, foam, plywood, or other unnaturally colored material from showing through the final ground cover. After the paint has thoroughly dried, use an artist's spatula to spread the goop about ⅛" thick over about a 1- to 2-square-foot area, **1**.

Sprinkle on different colors and textures of dirt, ground foam, and leaves, **2**. Once these are applied, mist the entire area with "wet water" (tap water with a drop or two of dishwashing liquid added), **3**. Wetting the area will usually reveal spots where there may not be enough dirt or foam to cover the goop. If that is the case simply spread more dirt and foam for thorough coverage.

Once these areas are re-wet, finish by applying a white glue-water mix (1 part glue to 1 part water) to the entire area with an eyedropper or pump sprayer, **4**.

Once everything is dry, simulate denser brush and bushes with polyfiber and buffing pads. Do this by first pulling the polyfiber and buffing pads into small pieces about an inch or two square. Then pull these apart even more, **5**. This will spread the material out and make it less dense. Place these on the ground, press them in place with your fingers, sprinkle fine-textured AMSI ground foam onto them, and fix it in place with a spritz of hairspray, **6**.

Spread "ground goop" on the base with an artist's spatula. The goop should have a consistency like peanut butter. Spread the mixture about ⅛" thick.

Depending upon the appearance you're trying to achieve, sprinkle a mix of dirt, ground foam, and leaves atop the ground goop.

Mist the area with "wet water." The detergent in the water will help the following glue mix better penetrate the scenery materials.

Fix the ground cover in place with a mix of thinned white glue (mixed 1:1 with water). Make sure the ground materials are thoroughly saturated.

Make taller brush and bushes with small pieces of polyfiber. Use your fingers to stretch and pull the polyfiber apart.

Sprinkle ground foam on the polyfiber, then fix the foam in place with a mist of hair spray.

CHAPTER FOUR

Making conifer trees

A spruce tree nicely frames this scene in the backyard of one of the company houses next door to the Peerless Tannery on my HO layout section.

Trees are everywhere in real life, and adding them to a model railroad will increase the realism of almost any scene. Even a small model railroad can use a lot of miniature trees, and fortunately for modelers there are a number of methods for building lots of trees in relatively short order.

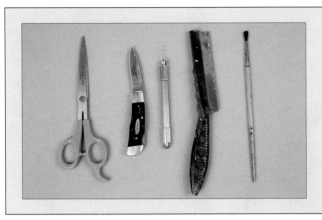

Tools:

- Scissors
- Pocket knife
- Pin vise
- Razor saw
- Small paintbrush

We'll start with a look at evergreens. The conifer family of evergreens consists of the pine, larch, spruce, hemlock, Douglas fir, and fir. They are all roughly conical in shape and all but the larch hold their needles year round (hence the term evergreen). The last five varieties are very easily modeled. If you want a better idea of what the different types of conifers look like and where they grow, you might want to pick up a copy of *Trees of North America* by Alan Mitchell. For a more in-depth study of trees in general, the *Textbook of Dendrology* by Harlow and Harrar (published by McGraw-Hill) might be the answer.

Two materials I find helpful for making evergreens are commercial buffing pads and home furnace filters. We'll look at making trees with those materials, along with using commercially available trees for highlighting detailed foreground scenes.

After trying numerous materials and methods over the years while attempting to come up with a good-looking miniature evergreen tree, I came to the conclusion that the buffing pad/furnace filter variety seemed to yield the most believable conifer tree for the least amount of time and effort.

I found four types of buffing pads that work well. They are all made by the Norton Company and are available at most well-stocked hardware stores. If you can't find them there, or if you decide to buy in bulk, Norton's contact information is on page 94. The first three pads, intended for the general public, are marketed under the Bear-Tex name and are 6" wide, 9" long, and ⅜" thick. The first type, green, is called a scouring pad. The next, brown, is a general-purpose pad. The third type, gray, is a hand pad. The fourth variety of pad, actually a disc, is intended for the commercial market. Referred to as scrubbing pads, they are from 13" to 23" in diameter and 1" thick. They are used to remove wax and sealant from floor tile. I am particularly fond of the general-purpose and gray-colored industrial types.

If you choose the furnace filter method, buy the cheapest, largest filters available at your local hardware store (it seems that regardless of size, they're always the same price). I strongly recommend using a number of pad types along with the furnace filters—each yields a slightly different appearance, and variety is what we are striving for.

Construction

When using furnace filters for foliage, begin by spraying the furnace filter with any cheap flat brown or gray paint, **1**. This step is unnecessary when using the brown or gray variety of buffing pads.

If you're modeling a larger foreground tree and the base of the trunk will show, use a ¼" to ⅜" square or round pine, basswood, or balsa stick and whittle one end to a point with a knife, **2**. Scribe bark texture into the trunk by drawing a razor saw along its surface, **3**. Drill a no. 55 hole in the base of the trunk with a pin vise and insert a length of floral wire, **4**. This will aid you in holding the tree during assembly and make planting it much easier. Bamboo skewers (available in most well-stocked super markets) can be used as trunks for smaller trees.

Materials:

- Bear-Tex:
  - General-purpose pad, 74700
  - Scouring pad, 79600
  - Hand pad, 85100
- Industrial scrubbing pad
- Furnace filters
- Quick Grab cement
- AMSI Conifer Green ground foam
- Assorted bamboo skewers
- Pine, balsa, or basswood stripwood
- Floral wire
- Minwax Special Walnut stain
- Rave Mega Hold no. 4 hairspray
- Flat brown spray paint

1

Spray furnace filters with inexpensive flat brown or gray aerosol paint.

2

Trunks can be made from balsa, basswood, or pine strips and rods. Whittle trunk tops to a point.

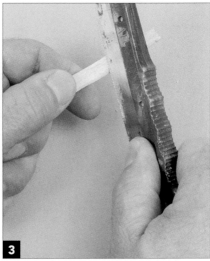

3

Scrape each trunk several times with a razor saw to create bark texture.

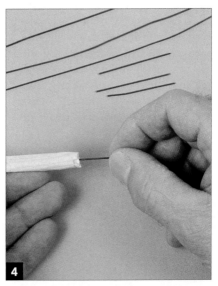

4

Drill a hole in the base of the trunk with a pin vise, then insert floral wire.

5

Stain each trunk. I prefer Minwax special walnut stain.

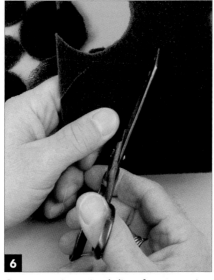

6

Cut out various-sized discs from scouring and buffing pads with scissors.

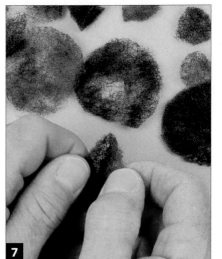

7

Tear discs apart and thin them out.

Simply cut them to various lengths and whittle the base to a point so they are easier to plant.

Stain tree trunks with before assembly, **5**. I use Minwax special walnut stain, but others will work as well. If you are planning to build a large number of trees it's easiest to pour the stain into a paint tray and soak the trunks rather than paint them individually. After the trunks have soaked for a few minutes, remove them from the tray and wipe them dry with a piece of cotton cloth.

Use scissors to cut the filters and pads into round discs of various diameters, **6**. Cut some into triangles to use as tops. Tear the discs into layers, making them as thin in cross section as possible, **7**. Pull the triangular pieces apart as well. This will give them an airy look.

Once you've accumulated a pile of discs and tips in many sizes, start impaling discs onto the trunks, working down from the top of each tree. Apply a small dab of Quick Grab glue to the trunk before installing each disc. Make the discs smaller toward the top, finishing with a triangular piece pressed onto the top of the tree, **8**.

Once satisfied with the shape of the tree, spray it with Mega Hold hairspray, **9**, and sprinkle on some Scenic Express

8

Press on discs, then the triangular top.

9

Coat the tree with hairspray.

10

Sprinkle on Scenic Express ground foam.

11

Save commercial trees for foreground use. Here an On30 train rolls past several tall Sterling Models white pines.

conifer or forest green fine textured ground foam, **10**.

While our homemade conifers will do for distant woods and in some cases even when viewed relatively close-up, thanks to our friends at Sterling Models, there is a better alternative for those times when our trees come under really close scrutiny. For a number of years Carol and Craig Freeland have been making a variety of evergreen trees that replicate their full scale counterparts better than anything else I've seen on the market.

Photo **11** shows a few of these trees in foreground use on my Sandy River & Rangeley Lakes On30 layout. Although these specimens would be a bit pricy for an entire forest, I often use them to highlight key scenes while filling the background with homemade trees.

CHAPTER FIVE

Realistic deciduous trees

Number 6184 rolls past the wood-lined road and yard of the Cobb farm in this HO scale scene.

Like conifers, different varieties of hardwood trees have distinct characteristics and shapes. Even though it is not necessary to replicate specific types of trees exactly, it does help to recognize the features of those common to the area you are modeling. Let's look at using some natural materials to duplicate them in miniature.

Since my previous HO scale West Hoosic Division Railroad and now my current O scale Sandy River Railroad are modeled after railroads of the Northeastern U. S., which is noted for its heavily wooded countryside, I am always looking for new and better ways to re-create those woodlands in miniature. This project covers the materials and construction techniques I have used to create some of my most realistic deciduous trees.

My three favorite raw materials for constructing deciduous trees in HO scale are spirea, oregano, and peppergrass, **1**. Spirea grows in abundance at the higher elevations of the Northeast. The plants grow in large clumps (2 to 3 feet in diameter) about 3 to 5 feet high. They can most often be found growing in open, abandoned farm fields.

In its wild state, oregano seems to inhabit the same type of areas as spirea, only at lower elevations. Wild oregano bushes also don't seem to grow as large as spirea. The individual plants will often be found in very small clumps, even single stalks, not over a foot or two in height. Oregano is actually an herb that has spread on its own to open fields in many northeastern states. My wife, Cheryl, found a large cache of the stuff in an empty lot as we walked along a residential street in the heart of Boston a number of years ago. If you prefer growing your own crop of oregano, it is certainly possible. The local nurseries in New York carry

a number of varieties. We had three plants we purchased, all growing like weeds (pardon the pun) in my former backyard. The part of the plant that is use to make our miniature trees is really the flower of the bush. It is best picked in mid-fall, when the stalks of the plant have died and are dried out and have turned brown.

The last plant I like to use for trees is peppergrass. Accumulating samples of this plant is a lot less adventuresome than the others, since it does not grow wild in either New York or the Carolinas. Fortunately, because of its popularity in dried flower arrangements, it can be found at almost

1

Several types of natural plants will make realistic miniature trees. My favorites are, from left, spirea, oregano, and peppergrass.

2

Once you have gathered enough of the branch material together, make a realistically thick trunk by wrapping the branches with floral tape.

3

Place a dab of glue on a length of floral wire (or other stiff wire) and stick the wire in the base of the trunk. This will make the tree much easier to mount in the scenery.

4

Spray the foliage with flat green aerosol paint. Any inexpensive brand will do—the key is choosing the proper color.

any well-stocked arts-and-crafts store (try Michaels) throughout the country. It is available dyed in a number of colors and is often referred to as "candy tuft." I usually buy mine in whatever shade of green is on hand, although, since I paint the stuff, it really doesn't matter what color it is.

The other materials I use for my tree-making endeavors are shown in the materials list. They include, from the local arts and crafts store, floral wrapping tape, floral wire, tube-type artist's acrylic paints, and plastic bottles of liquid acrylic craft paints. Tube

acrylics are a very thick consistency, much like oil paints, only they are water-soluble. Acrylic craft paints, such as Apple Barrel or Ceramcoat, are much more diluted but still thicker than model paint. They too are water soluble. Inexpensive green aerosol paint and a tube of Quick Grab glue come from the local hardware store.

For finishing colors, I use model paints from Floquil. Although Floquil and Polly Scale paints are no longer made, I still have an ample supply on hand. Feel free to substitute similar colors from any other model paint line.

For summer foliage I use coach green, Burlington Northern green, and reefer yellow. Be sure to use adequate ventilation when using aerosol paints, Floquil, or any other solvent-based paint.

Regardless of which type of material we use for our tree, begin by arranging a clump of sprigs (usually four or five) so they resemble the branch structure and crown of a real tree. Once you are satisfied with their configuration, wrap two or three layers of floral tape tightly around them, 2.

Apply some Quick Grab glue to a length of floral wire and insert it

5 Paint over the floral tape on the trunk with a couple of thick coats of artist's tube acrylic paint. As the first coat dries, pull the paint outward to form the top of the root structure at the base.

6 Airbrush the foliage to fine-tune the final color. You can use any of several green, yellow, and red model paints depending upon the final appearance you're looking for.

7 Use a soft-bristle brush to paint the trunk and all exposed branches with various shades of acrylic gray craft paint. A small palette is handy for mixing colors.

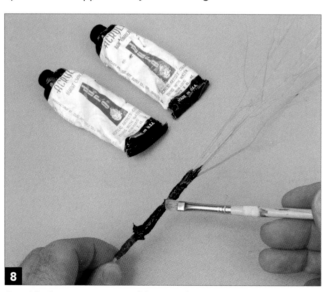

8 As with the green trees, add an acrylic-paint trunk to the branch structure of the dead tree.

into the bottom of the tree trunk, **3**. This will help you hold the tree while painting and placing it into position on the layout.

Once you have made a batch of trees, spray the foliage with inexpensive green aerosol paint, **4**. This step isn't absolutely necessary, but it will minimize the amount of finish painting needed later.

Let the initial application of paint dry for a couple hours. Apply tube acrylics to the trunk of the tree with a stiff-bristle artist's brush. Apply the paint along the trunk of the tree from

9 Spray-paint the entire tree with gray auto primer.

10 Save commercial trees, such as this Sterling Models HO scale maple, for foreground scenes. Fall colors can include various shades of orange, yellow, and red.

11 Here's a Sterling Models maple. This taller model is suitable for O scale.

the base of the crown to the bottom of the trunk. As the acrylic paint dries, pull strands of it out and away from the base of the trunk to create roots, **5**. It's only necessary to perform this step for foreground trees that might be under close scrutiny. The entire tree, including the trunk, will be painted later, but it's a good idea to use raw sienna, burnt umber, or various shades of gray in case any color shows through after final painting.

Once the tube acrylics have dried for a few hours, reach for your green foliage colors and airbrush, **6**. For summer foliage I use a mix of one part coach green, one part Burlington Northern green, and one to six parts Reefer Yellow. If you're aiming for fall

colors, try a mix of reefer yellow, reefer orange, and signal red.

The final step in preparing a tree is applying acrylic craft paints (in various shades of gray and brown) to the branches and trunk. Squeeze two or three colors into a paint tray and use a soft-bristle brush to apply them to the tree, working down from the branches to the base of the trunk. Blend the colors so the finished job doesn't appear monotone, **7**.

I also use Peppergass to represent smaller barren hardwoods in my O scale spring scenery. After defoliating the sprigs of Peppergrass and wrapping them together with foliage tape, add acrylic trunks, **8**, and paint them with gray primer, **9**, followed by a coating

of two teaspoons India ink to one pint alcohol.

As with the conifers we discussed in Chapter 4, when preparing a foreground scene where only really outstanding representations of actual trees will due, I again turn to Sterling Models. Regardless of what scale you are working in they produce an assortment of hardwood trees that really stand out when closely scrutinized. An example is the HO scale (early fall) maple in photo **10**. Standing a scale 37 feet tall (4½"), its leaves are just turning color. Although also an early fall example, the leaves on the 37-foot tall (9¼") O scale maple in photo **11** have not yet started to turn.

CHAPTER SIX

Super Trees and Super Sage

After years of reading, researching, and sharing information with other scenery junkies, I thought I had seen or tried just about all the ways there were to create a good-looking minia-ture hardwood tree for my model railroad. Then, I happened upon a Scenic Express catalog. Among the products in the catalog was a large assortment of different textures and colors of ground foam, Noch Leaf Flake Flocking, and an item called Super Trees. Not only did the Super Trees look great, they were also relatively easy to build.

Southern Railway Mikado No. 4836 crosses a plate girder bridge over the Sacco River. The HO scene includes trees and brush made from Super Trees and other products.

29

Tools:

- Scenic Express:
    Concentrated matte medium
    Spray Mister scenery sprayer
    Self-closing tweezers
- Large cooking tin
- Clothespins
- String
- Quick Grab glue
- Tweezers
- Grey Paint

Materials:

- Scenic Express:
    Super Sage material
    Super Tree material
    Noch olive green leaves
    Noch light green leaves
    Noch mid-green leaves

After soaking the tree in diluted matte medium, sprinkle flocking in place. Use a pan or box to capture and reuse stray flocking.

Use clothespins to clip trees upside-down to a string "clothesline" until dry. Hanging another clothespin or two to the top of the tree will help straighten crooked tree trunks. Lightly mist them with diluted matte medium to help secure the flocking.

Most importantly, the colors used for the foams and flocking marketed by Scenic Express were an exact match to the AMSI ground foams and Floquil paints I had been using for the grass, brush, and tree foliage on my HO scale West Hoosic Division. The varieties of Scenic Express ground foam that are compatible with my materials are light green, grass green, spring green, summer lawn, and farm pasture blend. These could be spread on my miniature hills and dales to replicate either grass or weeds (see Chapter 3). The fine conifer green works great for foliage on handmade conifer trees (Chapter 4).

3 Along with Super Sage, you'll need caulk, floral tape, flat gray spray paint, diluted India ink, and acrylic paints.

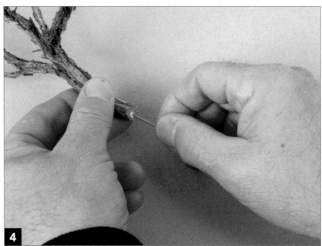

4 Glue a length of brass wire into the base of the trunks to make the trees easier to mount.

5 Apply latex caulk to the base of the trunk, then shape it to represent the visible root structure. Waxed paper atop a foam base makes the job easier.

6 Trim the small branch structure from the Super Tree material for application to the coarser Super Sage tree structure.

Finally, they carry a line of Noch Leaf Flake Flock that, when used on the branch structure of Super Trees, creates a miniature hardwood tree that's really hard to beat.

The Super Tree branch and trunk structure is all one piece. Actually, the skeletal component of Super Trees is a wild growth called filigrane. According to the folks at Scenic Express you can only find this stuff in high, rocky regions of Scandinavia. If your passport has expired, just order it by the bag from Scenic Express. The trees come in large 12" x 15" plastic bags with enough material to make 50 to 100 trees, depending on their size.

You can apply ground foam to the tree structure if you like, but I think the Noch Leaf Flake Flock makes

much more realistic leaves. The three varieties that blend best with my other scenery materials are mid green, light green, and olive green.

Making a tree

To make a batch of Super Trees, begin by stringing a "clothesline" of heavy string about 10 feet long across your work area. Fill a basin with diluted matte medium (purchase it pre-diluted or make your own mix of 1 part matte medium to 5 parts water). After using a hobby knife to remove the small leaves attached to the stems, fully immerse some of the trees in the matte medium and let them soak for at least 30 seconds.

Remove each tree from the matte medium, using tweezers to grasp it

near the center of the trunk. Holding the tree upright, sprinkle on the leaf flocking from above, carefully working your way around the tree, **1**.

Turn the tree upside down, clip it to the clothesline with a clothespin, remove the tweezers, and let the tree dry upside down. If a tree is particularly crooked, gently clip another clothespin to the top of the tree to pull it straight. Once you have a bunch of the trees hanging out to dry, give them all a misting of diluted matte medium in the pump spray bottle to help secure the foliage, **2**.

O scale hardwoods

For a heavier trunk and branch structure in HO (and especially O scale), I use Scenic Express Super Sage

7

Apply adhesive to the Super Sage branches. I used a product called Amazing Goop, made by Eclectic Products. This glue will securely hold the added branches.

8

Use tweezers to attach the fine Super Tree branches to the Super Sage tree structure.

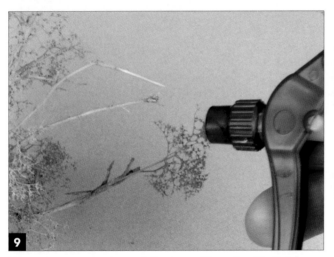

9

Use a pump sprayer to coat the tree with a mix of India ink diluted in alcohol.

10

The trees in this HO scene are made from a mix of Super Trees and Super Sage material.

sagebrush for the heavier branches and trunk portion of a tree in combination with sprigs of Super Trees to create the smaller branch structure. In fact, if you purchase an economy size box of Super Sage it comes with a separate box of Super Trees to create the finer branch structure along with a "how-to" flier in which Dave Frary explains the technique. Since I was now modeling early spring, my O scale hardwood trees had no foliage, so it wasn't necessary to add leaves to the branches.

One step not covered in the Scenic Express instructions is adding a root system to the trees. I used Jane's Trains technique for this step. After first drilling a hole in the base of the trunks with a no. 55 bit I glued a length of brass wire in place with a drop of Weld

Bond, **4**, and pressed the tree onto a sheet of foam with a piece of waxed paper sandwiched between the base of the tree and the foam.

After squeezing a glob of white acrylic household caulk on a piece of cardboard, I used a skewer stick to apply the caulk around the base of the sagebrush trunk, **5**. After the caulk had dried overnight, I removed the tree from the Styrofoam, peeled back the waxed paper, trimmed the roots with scissors, and painted them reefer gray. I spackled on dabs of black, raw umber, and burnt umber acrylics with a stiff bristle brush until the roots blended with the tree trunk color.

Next I used tweezers to trim away the small leaves that are inherently present on the Super Tree material,

then trimmed off the smaller branches from the Super Tree stems, **6**. After applying Amazing Goop adhesive to the sage branches, **7**, I used tweezers to attach the small segments of Super Tree material to the sage, **8**.

Once all the Super Tree branch extensions were applied, I sprayed them first with gray auto primer, then again with a pump sprayer filled with a mix of one teaspoon India ink to one pint rubbing alcohol, **9**. This darkened the gray, brought out highlights, and made the smaller branches blend better with the Super Sage trunk.

I left my early spring trees like this, but for a summer effect you can apply flocking as with Super Trees by dipping the branch structure in diluted matte medium and applying flocking, **10**.

CHAPTER SEVEN

Ground leaves for a forest floor

If you've ever walked through a forest, you've probably noticed one feature of the forest floor that really stands out—dead leaves. Every fall as hardwood trees go into hibernation, they drop their leaves in the process. After losing their color and dropping from the trees, leaves turn various shades of brown and carpet the forest floor until they decompose and are replaced the following season by a new batch. This constant revitalization creates a brown carpet of decomposing leaves year round.

Beyond the main line at Strong on my On30 layout, we see coarse ground hardwood leaves under the trees and underbrush at left. To the right are ground up pine needles around the base of the Sterling Models pine trees.

Here's a bag of full scale dead leaves. The price is right, and they can be found just about everywhere. Make sure they're dry if you're going to store them.

Start by filling the blender about half full with leaves. Remove the stems and any debris.

Tools and materials:

- Water bucket
- Dead leaves
- Tap water
- Kitchen sieve
- Spatula
- Cotton T-shirt
- Cookie sheets
- Electric blender

One day, the members of the Tree Group (three other scenery junkies and I, who get together in an interactive modeling group) were discussing what we could use to create the look of dead leaves on the ground of our miniature woodlands. We decided that nothing could replicate dead leaves better than—you guessed it—dead leaves. All we had to do was come up with an efficient way to reduce them in scale. We found the answer to our dilemma at the local K-Mart store: an inexpensive blender. (Preserving our marriages precluded using any blenders we already had on hand.) The one we picked was a six-speed Sunbeam (model 4143), and we paid less than $20 for it. I'm sure you can find a comparable model from other manufacturers and stores.

Begin by raking and collecting a couple bags of leaves, **1**. It's best to do this after a spell of dry weather so the leaves are not wet, as damp leaves may rot during storage. If you are going to grind them right away, you don't have to worry about them being dry.

To grind the leaves, first remove the heavier stems and any dirt or other debris. Place the leaves in the blender, filling it about half way, **2**. Add water to the top of the leaves, **3**, and place the cover on the blender. Turn the blender

to frappé (medium/high) for about a minute, **4**.

Using an old cotton T-shirt as a filter, place it across the top of a bucket and pour the resulting mess into it, **5**. After letting it drain for a few minutes, wrap the shirt around the mix and squeeze out as much water as possible.

To dry the leaves quickly, spread the mix on an old cookie sheet, **6**, and place it in the oven. Set the oven temperature to 200 degrees Fahrenheit and leave the door ajar about 2 or 3 inches. This allows moisture to escape as the leaves are heated. To speed up drying time, use a spatula to turn the leaves occasionally, **7**.

You can also just let the leaves dry naturally by spreading the leaves out on some newspapers and letting them air-dry.

Once the leaves are completely dry, run them through a kitchen sieve or old window screen to filter out the finer-textured material, **8**. Separate the screened and unscreened leaves and store them separately. As you will see in projects throughout this book, both can be used in making scenery.

You'll also notice pine needles under the pine trees in the photo on page 33. I use exactly the same technique as leaves for grinding pine needles that I spread under my O scale pine trees.

Add plain tap water to the leaves. Fill the blender to the level of the top of the leaves.

Place the lid on the blender, select "frappe," and turn it on for one minute.

Pour the resulting mixture through an old T-shirt as a filter over a water bucket.

Squeeze out as much water as possible and spread the ground-up leaves on a cookie tray.

Place the cookie sheet in an oven set to 200 degrees Fahrenheit. Turn the leaf mixture occasionally with a spatula to speed the drying process and prevent clumping.

This view shows unfiltered leaves in the middle, filtered ones on the left, and pine needles on the right.

CHAPTER EIGHT

Turning trees into a forest

Wander east from the HO scale Peerless Tannery and you'll quickly be in the thick woods. A realistic forest requires more than simply planting a group of trees in the ground.

If you have been tackling the projects in this book sequentially, you know how to make your own ground cover and dead leaves. You also can whip together both conifer and hardwood trees. Now it's time to combine all of these techniques and create a finished forest scene.

Tools:

- 1"-wide, soft-bristle brush
- Artist's spatula
- Teaspoon
- Awl
- Tweezers
- Scissors
- Pump sprayer for "wet water"
- Pump sprayer for matte medium (or diluted white glue)

Besides the materials shown in the photo at right, you will need a supply of "wet water" (tap water with a few drops of dishwashing liquid added), diluted matte medium or white glue (5 parts water to one part concentrated matte medium or 3 parts water to 1 part glue), and an assortment of hardwoods, conifers, and Super Trees. It usually takes about 30 assorted sizes and types of trees to fill a 1-square-foot area in HO while in O scale they will cover 4 or 5 square feet. This will vary according to how thick you want your woods to appear.

HO woodlot

When working in HO, begin by pre-painting the scenery base with full-strength flat earth-tone latex house paint. Next, use a spatula to spread a ⅛"-thick layer of "ground goop" mix (see Chapter 3) over an area approximately 2 feet square, **1**. Cover

Materials:

- Flat earth-color paint (Pittsburgh Tobacco Brown interior flat latex paint, 7607, or similar)
- Matte medium (If using a concentrate, dilute 1 part medium to 5 parts water.)
- Ground goop mix: 1 cup Celluclay, 1 cup Vermiculite, 1 cup earth-color latex paint, ⅔ cup white glue, and one capful concentrated Lysol disinfectant
- Assorted textures of dirt
- Twigs
- Coarse- and fine-ground leaves (see Chapter 7)
- Small rocks
- Assorted textures and colors of ground foam
- "Wet water" (tap water with a few drops of dishwashing liquid added)

1

Paint the scenery base with earth-color paint, then spread "ground goop" over the base.

2

Add small rocks and outcroppings, then use a spoon to sprinkle coarse dirt around the rocks.

3

Add twigs and fine branches, then spread coarse and fine dried leaves across the area.

4

Spray the entire scene with "wet water" and then with diluted matte medium or diluted white glue.

5

Plant the brush by poking a hole with an awl, dipping the stem in white glue, and sticking it in place.

6

With ground cover in place, add trees by gluing their mounting wires in small holes in the goop.

the goop with various textures of sifted dirt. Press some larger stones into the goop, then build up additional goop around them to make them look as if they're embedded in the soil and jutting out of the hills.

Sprinkle some very coarse dirt around the stone outcroppings to resemble loose gravel that has been worn away and exposed by the elements, **2**. Add various textures and colors of fine dirt and ground foam. Randomly place twigs into the Goop to represent fallen branches and small trees, then add coarse and fine ground

leaves to the entire scene, **3**. Once you're satisfied with the overall effect, spray everything with "wet water" and diluted matte medium or diluted white glue until the area is thoroughly saturated, **4**. The detergent in the water cuts its surface tension, allowing the glue or matte medium to better penetrate the materials. Reapply more dirt, foam, and dried leaves to any bare areas that appear, then lightly re-spray everything with more matte medium or glue.

The branch structure of Super Trees, nicely represents brush. You can accumulate brush samples by trimming the

individual branches off the stems of the previously prepared Super Trees with a pair of scissors. To install the Super Tree brush, punch a hole in the Goop with a small awl and, after dipping the brush into full-strength white glue, push it in place, **5**.

After adding the brush to the scene, dip the different types and sizes of hardwood and conifer trees into the white glue and press them into the goop at random, **6**. Add Super Tree branches around the perimeter of the woods to represent the secondary growth and brush that thrives in that area, **7**.

7 Plant additional Super Tree brush around the perimeter of the woods.

8 Start with fine ground cover, then add an assortment of twigs and brush to the forest floor.

9 Once the ground cover is in place, begin planting trees. This O scale forest is set in early spring, before the leaves have begun popping out on deciduous trees.

10 A trainman stands at the edge of the forest as he waits to throw the switch on this On30 scene.

O scale woods

Now let me explain how we slapped together an early spring scene for the On30 sectional layout. Besides the defoliated smaller Peppergrass trees we made in Chapter 5 and the larger Super Tree-Super Sage varieties we built in Chapter 6, my wife, Cheryl, and I went on a mini-tree hunt on the back roads around our home. We found wild oregeno, picked up sticks, and clipped sprigs from various bushes growing along the road right of way that looked like they might resemble full-grown trees and brush in

O scale. Next we headed for the local Michaels craft store. There we found an assortment of material in the dried flower section, including candy tuft and other materials designed for floral arrangements.

Some gray-painted Super Tree branches, along with wild oregano and sprigs of various dry foliage obtained during our Michaels trip would represent the low brush found growing beneath the larger trees in and around the edge of the forest. I didn't bother to paint the oregano or other dried materials, opting to use them in their

as-is state instead. This adds some subtle variation in color and texture to the scene.

I built up this forest just as I did in the HO version, by painting the scenery base, spreading ground goop over the area and adding dirt, stones, leaves, twigs, and bushes, **8**, before planting the larger trees, **9**. Note in the photos that since I was modeling early spring I stayed away from the green tones of foam I used in the HO scene and used more dirt and dead leaves as ground cover. Photo **10** shows the finished scene.

CHAPTER NINE

Rock formations from Foam Putty

An auto passes a rock outcropping as an HO scale Boston & Maine RS-3 eases across the Maple Street crossing.

For years I've been reading about various ways to replicate rock outcroppings in miniature using different types of plaster. Unfortunately, when you make rock outcroppings for your model railroad with plaster, they weigh almost as much as the rocks you're trying to re-create! Woodland Scenics came to the rescue with a product they call Foam Putty.

Tools:

- Putty knife
- Woodland Scenics Foam Knife
- Soft-bristle brush (wide) for removing excess foam cuttings
- Assorted small soft-bristle brushes to apply acrylics
- Small stiff-bristle brush to apply pastels

Materials:

- Woodland Scenics Foam Putty
- Raw sienna tube acrylic
- Raw umber tube acrylic
- Mars black tube acrylic
- Weber/Costello: Hi-Fi Gray pastels Earth Tone pastels

Foam Putty comes in 16-ounce containers and is part of the company's Subterrain Lightweight Layout System. Foam Putty looks and handles like spackling compound, but weighs about a third as much. It can be used to fill cracks between foam sheets, build grades for roads, provide smooth sub-surfaces for structures, and, most importantly for us, create rock outcroppings. The material is compatible with other scenery base materials, not just foam.

Foam Putty can be applied with a putty knife and carved with a knife. When dry, it can be colored with the same acrylic paints that we use on plaster rocks and other scenery.

Start by globbing generous amounts of Foam Putty on the scenic base where you want an outcropping, **1**. After allowing the putty to dry thoroughly (about two days), use

Determine where you want a rock outcropping, then use a putty knife to spread generous amounts of Foam Putty on the scenic base.

After the Foam Putty dries, use a foam knife to carve it to the shape of a rock formation.

Remove any residue with a soft brush.

Start the coloring process by applying a wash of raw sienna acrylic paint to the entire rock formation.

Apply a wash of raw umber acrylic paint after the initial coat of raw sienna has dried.

Finish with a coat of thinned Mars black. The black will settle in crevices and highlight shadow areas.

Brush on various colors of pastel chalks to highlight some of the rocks.

a knife—I highly recommend the Woodland Scenics Foam Knife— to remove any unnatural-looking formations and carve rock outcroppings into the putty, 2.

There's no right or wrong way to do this, and the putty will work to form different kinds of rocks. Sedimentary rocks will have more texture and can show layers; igneous or metamorphic rocks might be larger and more defined in shape. If in doubt, look at the real

thing (or photos of real rocks) for ideas. Remove any trimmed residue with a soft-bristle brush, 3.

Artist's tube acrylics work well for coloring the Foam Putty rockwork. Squeeze about 1" of each acrylic color (raw sienna, raw umber, and Mars black) into three paper cups—one color per cup. Add about a tablespoon of water to the first two colors and three tablespoons to the black. Begin by applying raw sienna, 4. Next, use

a clean brush to apply raw umber, 5. Follow with an application of Mars black to highlight deep recesses and shadows, 6.

Once the initial application is complete, highlight any splotchy colors until you're satisfied with the overall effect. After the acrylics have dried, brush on assorted colors of Earth Tone and Hi-Fi Gray pastels, 7. Adjust the paint and chalk colors as needed, again following prototype photos.

CHAPTER TEN

Creating wetlands in four easy stages

Swamps and other small, still bodies of water are common along the tracks throughout the country. Here an HO Rutland Alco glides past a boat pulled to the shore of a pond.

Although commonly seen in nature, swamps and bogs are scenic features that most model railroaders tend to avoid replicating. I had a couple of swamps on my HO West Hoosic Division, and I think both were pretty realistic representations of the real thing. Let's follow the four-stage process I used to create my miniature wetlands.

Apply plaster gauze over the swamp area and up the neighboring banks.

STAGE 1: SCENIC BASE

Make a foam base for the water following Chapter 1's guidelines. The water area should be a flat piece of foam, with banks sloping down to it. Lightly spray the foam with some "wet water" (tap water with a few drops of dishwashing liquid added), then apply plaster gauze, **1**. Add a couple layers of (soaked) plaster gauze around the perimeter and onto the bottom of the swamp area. When the plaster dries, use a soft-bristle brush to apply a coating of full-strength earth-color latex paint to the area surrounding the swamp, **2**. Squeeze out some full-strength raw umber tube acrylic paints. Use a stiff paintbrush (one made for artist's oil paints) to blend the acrylic and tan latex earth paint to create a murky brown color, **3**. Now apply full-strength black tube acrylics to the deepest areas of the swamp. Blend the black with the raw umber to create the illusion of depth to the Enviro-Tex water you'll apply later, **4**. After the paint dries, apply a layer of "ground goop" mix (see Chapter 3) up to the edge of the swamp, **5**.

Apply earth-color latex paint down the edges of the banks to the edge of the water surface area.

Blend raw umber and black acrylic paints with the earth-tone paint with a flat artist's brush.

Continue blending the acrylics across the water bed, making the darkest areas in the middle. This will create the illusion of depth when the water is applied.

Apply a layer of ground goop to the surrounding terrain and down the banks to the edge of the swamp or water area.

Stage 1 Tools:

- Scenic Express Spray Mister for applying water
- Soft-bristle, 1"-wide brush for latex paint
- Artist's spatula, for applying ground goop
- Stiff-bristle oil paintbrush, for artist's acrylics

Stage 1 Materials:

- Dishpan for water
- Raw umber tube acrylic paint
- Burnt umber tube acrylic paint
- Black tube acrylic paint
- Pittsburgh Tobacco Brown interior flat latex wall paint, 7607
- Ground goop (See Chapter 3)
- Woodland Scenics plaster cloth
- Woodland Scenics assorted Subterrain foam panels

STAGE 2: GROUND COVER

After planting various trees in the wooded lot surrounding the swamp, use a spoon to spread a thick layer of coarse leaf material onto the swamp base. Next, sprinkle fine-textured dried leaf material around the shallow wet areas of the swamp, **6**. It will represent a murky residue. Once you're satisfied with the appearance, cover the entire area with a light spray of diluted matte medium, **7**. Since some species of conifer (mainly spruce and hemlock) proliferate around damp areas like swamps, plant some buffing-pad evergreens here and there for effect, **8**. Use small chunks of buffing-pad material to create the thick brush found around the perimeter of your swamp.

Cut small clumps of branches from the stems of Super Trees and use an awl to jab a hole in the ground goop. Dip the branches in some Weld Bond and plug them into the hole with a pair of tweezers, **9**. Now sprinkle the area with AMSI foam and add Woodland Scenics flowers (sparingly) to the surface of the buffing pads applied earlier around the perimeter of the swamp, **10**. Finally, use a spritz of hairspray to hold these textures in place, **11**.

Spread fine and coarse leaves around the perimeter of the swamp area.

Stage 2 Tools:

- Teaspoon
- Awl
- Tweezers
- Pump-style hairspray
- Scenic Express Spray Mister for applying diluted matte medium

Stage 2 Materials:

- Weld Bond glue
- Coarse and fine-texture ground-up dried leaves
- Assorted twigs
- Woodland Scenics:
  Polyfiber mesh
  Blended turf foam
  Flowers
- AMSI:
  Spring green foam (fine)
  Spring green foam (coarse)
  Yellow green foam (fine)
  Yellow green foam (coarse)
  Grass green foam (fine)
  Grass green foam (coarse)
- Scenic Express:
  Super Trees

Once the ground cover is in place, spray it with a mist of diluted matte medium.

Plant some buffing-pad conifers and use small pieces of pad material to make thick brush in some areas.

Place twigs around the swamp area. Poke holes in the ground and plant Super Tree material to represent brush and scrub.

Fill in areas with ground foam as needed, then sprinkle on (sparingly) Woodland Scenics foam flowers.

Fix the twigs, scrub, and brush in place with a spritz of hairspray.

Stage 3 Tools:

- Tweezers
- Scissors
- Pump-style hairspray

Stage 3 Materials:

- Weld Bond glue
- Assorted brushes (from arts-and-crafts shop)
- Air fern (from craft or flower shop)
- Caspia (from craft or flower shop)
- Woodland Scenics: Field grass (medium green, light green, and harvest gold)

STAGE 3: SWAMP GRASS

To replicate the tall swamp grass and weeds that grow in the water, start by clumping three varieties (colors) of Woodland Scenics field grass together. Grasp the resulting bunch between your thumb and forefinger, then trim off (square) one end of the grass with scissors, **12**. Shift the bunch to your other hand, then cut off a grass clump about ¼" long and dip it in Weld Bond, **13**.

With the glue-dipped end facing downward, place the clump in position in your swamp. Once it's in place, gently tap the top of the grass to spread it apart, **14**. You can use the same technique for planting the broom material, but only trim one end of each clump. This gives the broom bushes an uneven top and thus adds visual interest.

Plant individual sprigs of air fern and caspia using a similar technique. Start by using scissors to trim off some small branches. Use tweezers to dip the air fern in Weld Bond and plant it in the swamp among the field and broom grass, **15**. Adding a dead tree made from a twig finishes the scene, **16**.

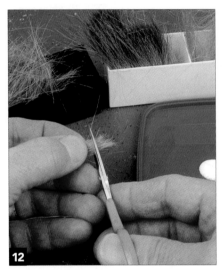

Hold a clump of Woodland Scenics grass and trim it evenly.

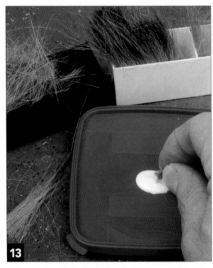

Dip the end of the grass clump in Weld Bond adhesive.

After the grass is planted and secured, tap the tops to spread the strands.

15

16

Dip pieces of air fern in Weld Bond and use tweezers to plant them among the Woodland Scenics grass.

A fallen dead tree (taken from a fine branch of a real tree) is a nice finishing touch to the ground cover.

STAGE 4: SWAMP WATER

Measure equal parts of the Enviro-Tex polymer resin and hardener in hot-grade paper cups. Thoroughly mix the resin in another cup. Failing to mix the components completely will result in uncured resin and a huge mess of ruined scenery.

Carefully pour the resin onto the swamp base, **17**. Capillary action will spread it among the previously planted weeds and grass. Make sure your water area is completely sealed (especially at the edge of a layout), as Enviro-Tex will find any stray opening or hole after you pour it.

Gently exhale across the surface of the resin to draw any air bubbles to the surface. The Enviro-Tex takes about 72 hours to cure fully, **18**.

The lily pads floating on the water are actually peppergrass leaves. Once the epoxy had thoroughly dried, I pulled the leaves from a branch of peppergrass with tweezers, dipped them one at a time in a puddle of white glue, and placed them on the surface of the epoxy water.

17

Carefully pour the mixed resin onto the base of the swamp. Capillary action will pull it into the weeded areas.

Stage 4 Tools:
- Craft sticks
- Stopwatch
- Paper cups

18

Exhale on the swamp surface to get air bubbles out of the Enviro-Tex.

CHAPTER ELEVEN

Making a mill pond

This rear of the HO Peerless Tanning Company is reflected in the still water of a mill pond. You can use these techniques for ponds, rivers, lakes, and other bodies of water.

One of the most interesting "real world" scenic features for model railroaders to replicate is water. In the early to mid-20th century, mills and mill ponds were plentiful. You can use the same techniques to make other types of waterways in any scale.

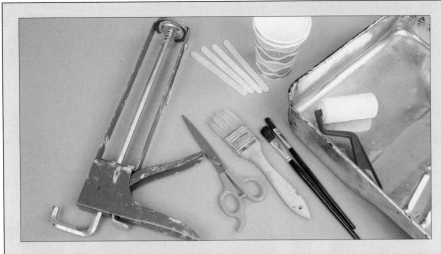

Tools:

- Scissors
- Small paint roller and paint pan
- Medium-size soft-bristle brush, for applying earth-tone paint
- Caulk gun
- Small soft-bristle brushes, for feathering earth-tone and black paints along pond edge
- Paper cups
- Craft sticks, for stirring epoxy

Materials:

- Woodland Scenics:
    Plaster cloth
    Foam sheets
- Pan for water
- Pittsburgh:
    Tobacco Brown interior flat latex paint, 7607
    Semigloss black interior paint, 7757
- Latex primer
- Dap Dynaflex 230 indoor-outdoor clear latex sealant
- Evergreen Scale Models clear .010" styrene
- Enviro-Tex Lite polymer coating
- Styrene cement
- Weld Bond glue

Mill ponds were usually created by damming a stream. These ponds served a number of purposes. They supplied water for the manufacturing process, water for fire protection, and, finally, water to turn the turbines that powered the machinery in the mill. Since those mills were often served by railroads, it was a given that a number of mills and ponds should be included on my 1950s Boston & Maine model railroad.

For this project, I decided not only to build a mill pond but also a waterfall flowing over a dam along with a cascading stream. The construction of the scenery base for the pond and stream were covered in Chapter 1, and many of the water techniques build upon those shown in Chapter 10.

Since this is a relatively complicated endeavor, I'm going to divide it into two parts. This chapter will explain how to create the pond, install the mill and dam, pour resin pond water, and complete the initial stages of the pond outfall. I decided to have my pond bordered on two sides by woods and on two sides by the large mill (Peerless Leather) and dam, **1**.

I had already lined the bottom of the pond with ⅛"-thick Masonite to protect the foam panels from the Enviro-Tex water and provide a smooth surface for the bottom of the pond. After cutting foam panels to fit around the perimeter of the Masonite, use Weld Bond to glue them in place, **2**. Cover these panels with a double layer

of Woodland Scenics plaster gauze so that they, too, will be protected from the Enviro-Tex. Dip the strips of plaster gauze in water for a minute or two and apply them over the foam panels. Rub the surface of the cloth to help activate the impregnated plaster, **3**. Use a small paint roller to spread latex primer onto the pond base. When the primer coat is dry, use a roller to apply a smooth coat of black paint, **4**.

Next, brush-paint the ground around the pond perimeter and under the mill with earth-tone latex paint, **5**. Where the hillside meets the pond water, carry the brown out into the pond for about an inch.

While waiting for the paint to dry, apply a bead of clear latex caulk

1

My mill building includes the foundation and dam. The scenery base (layers of foam, see Chapter 1) was designed to fit this particular structure.

2

Glue the contoured foam banks in place surrounding the flat hardboard pond surface.

3

Dip lengths of plaster cloth in water, then add two layers of the material to the banks alongside the pond. Rub them with your fingers to smooth the surface.

4

Use a small paint roller to spread an even coat of black paint across the entire pond surface.

5

After the black paint dries, brush earth-color latex on the surrounding surface and about an inch onto the pond.

6

Apply a bead of clear caulk to the entire base of the mill. This DAP latex caulk goes on white, but dries clear. The caulk keeps the Enviro-Tex from seeping under the structure.

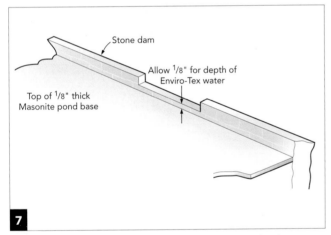

Stone dam

Allow 1/8" for depth of Enviro-Tex water

Top of 1/8" thick Masonite pond base

7

This shows how the hardboard pond base meets the dam. Allow ⅛" for the depth of the Enviro-Tex. The water will then appear to be pouring through the slot in the dam.

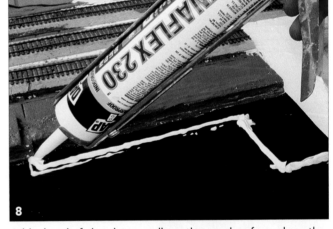

8

Add a bead of clear latex caulk on the pond surface where the structure and dam will go. Also run a bead of caulk where the pond surface meets the inside vertical surface of the dam.

around the base of the mill building where it will meet the resin water, **6**. This prevents any resin from seeping underneath the building. Apply a bead of caulk onto the pond base just inside the building walls as an additional barrier. Run another bead of caulk along the upper edge of the dam and place the dam into position so the spillway is ⅛" above the surface of the Masonite, **7, 8**. Once all the caulk is applied, place the dam and mill into position, **9**. Make sure there are no gaps for the water to escape.

Apply ground goop (see Chapter 3) and various textures of foam and dirt up to the edge of the pond. Fix everything in place with matte medium. After finishing the scenery, apply another generous coat of black paint up to the previously painted earth color. Using a second brush, immediately reapply earth-color paint, blending the two colors to create a soft edge transition from one to the other, **10**. Apply a coat of color to the base of the streambed that will eventually be filled with cascading (resin) water

below the pond, **11**. At this point, also cut a piece of .010" clear styrene, **12**, to serve as a base for the waterfall flowing over the dam. Glue the styrene to the spillway of the dam using some liquid plastic cement, **13**. We will attach it to the streambed later.

Thoroughly mix a batch of Enviro-Tex according to instructions (1 part resin, 1 part hardener). Pour the resin into the pond until it reaches the top of the outfall, **14**, and let it dry for a few days. Chapter 12 shows how to pour and finish the waterfall and stream.

Place the mill and dam into position. Make sure there are no gaps in the caulk where Enviro-Tex could escape.

Blend the black and earth-color paints at the pond edge to simulate depth.

Paint the base of the streambed with earth-color paint.

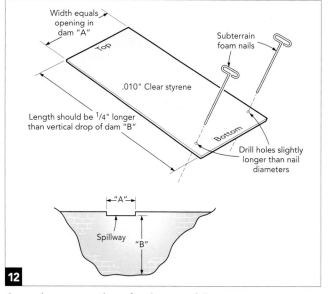

Width equals opening in dam "A"

Top

.010" Clear styrene

Length should be 1/4" longer than vertical drop of dam "B"

Subterrain foam nails

Bottom

Drill holes slightly longer than nail diameters

"A"

Spillway

"B"

Cut a clear styrene base for the waterfall.

Glue the clear styrene waterfall base to the spillway gap at the top of the dam.

Mix and pour the Enviro-Tex resin, covering the pond surface.

CHAPTER TWELVE

Pouring a mill stream

A Rutland train rolls across a stream and a highway on a multi-span deck girder bridge. Simulating flowing water, as in this HO scene, will add a nice touch of realism to almost any model railroad.

As I mentioned in Chapter 11, mill ponds were almost always created by damming an existing stream. For this reason it seemed only logical that I should have some sort of cascading stream leading away from the mill pond. You can follow these guidelines in making almost any kind of river or stream.

Tools:

- Woodland Scenics:
  - Foam Knife
  - Foam Nails
- Medium paintbrush, for applying earth-color latex paint
- Artist's spatula
- Teaspoon
- Fine-mesh kitchen sieve
- Pump sprayers
- Stiff-bristle brushes, for applying gloss medium and latex caulk
- Wood stirrers, for Enviro-Tex
- "Hot" paper cups, for Enviro-Tex
- Toothpicks, for applying epoxy
- Caulk gun

Materials:

- Woodland Scenics Plaster Cloth (gauze)
- Brown latex paint, such as Pittsburgh Tobacco Brown interior flat latex paint (no. 7607)
- Ground goop mix: 1 cup vermiculite, 1 cup Celluclay, 1 cup earth-color latex paint, ⅓ cup white glue, 1 capful of concentrated liquid Lysol, and water
- "Wet" water (tap water with a few drops of dishwashing liquid added)
- Scenic Express matte medium (if it's concentrated, mix 5 parts water to 1 part medium)
- Dark-color dirt
- Five-minute epoxy
- DAP Dynaflex:
  - 230 clear latex caulk
  - 230 white latex caulk
- Lexel clear Super Elastic sealant
- Liquitex medium-viscosity acrylic gloss medium
- Enviro-Tex resin
- Shallow pan

Since I was already using real dirt and small chunks of rocks in combination with "ground goop" to make rock outcroppings in my scenery (see Chapter 8), I felt that using real rocks for my streambed wouldn't be that difficult. After all, hand-carved or molded plaster rocks weigh almost as much as the real thing, and you have the additional challenge of coloring plaster to match the surrounding terrain. By using real rocks in combination with talus from the same source, it would be possible to have everything blend together naturally.

I found the rocks for my stream jutting out of a hillside along a county

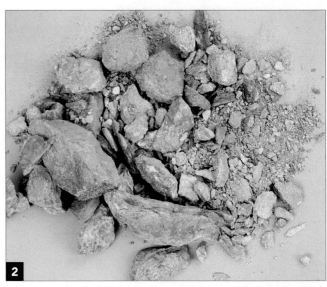

You can "mine" raw materials from fields, rock outcroppings, gravel roads, highway shoulders, back yards, and any number of other outdoor locations.

Get materials of all sizes, from gravel dust to larger rocks. Rock color varies by region—look at prototype photos for ideas and guidelines.

Test-fit the larger rocks along the streambed. A quick digital-camera or cellphone snapshot will help you remember where they all go in the following steps.

Remove the rocks, seal the riverbed with plaster gauze and paint the gauze with your earth-tone paint.

road about 20 miles from my old house in upstate New York. I filled a five-gallon bucket with the raw materials for the streambed, **1**. If you look at that photo closely, you can see how rain and erosion have caused the rock outcropping at the upper left to disintegrate and wash down the slope below. Remember, you want not only larger rocks but also the talus or eroded material, **2**.

Start developing the streambed by placing rocks into position at the waterfalls and various locations along the edge of the stream, **3**. Remove the

rocks and seal the riverbed with plaster gauze. After the gauze dries, paint over it with earth-color latex paint, **4**.

Apply "ground goop" (follow the formula in Chapter 3) with an artist's spatula over the streambed and about 3" or 4" up the sides of the surrounding hillsides, **5**. Press larger rocks into the wet goop, **6**. Now use a spoon to spread smaller stones and rubble around the larger rocks at the sides of the stream and at the various waterfalls, **7**. After sifting some of the eroded material through a fine kitchen sieve, use a spoon to spread it over the bed of the

stream. Add the darker dirt to enhance the illusion of water depth, **8**.

Once everything is in place, use a pump sprayer to apply "wet" water (water with a few drops of dish detergent added) over the entire area. While the scene is still wet, thoroughly saturate the entire area with matte medium, **9**. Let everything dry for a couple days.

Pin the clear styrene waterfall (see Chapter 11) to the streambed with foam nails and secure it with five-minute epoxy, **10**. Remove the nails after the epoxy has dried.

Apply "ground goop" along the streambed. An artist's spatula works well for applying the material. The color and texture of the goop look realistic and will hold other materials in place.

Place the larger rocks first, pressing them firmly into the ground goop.

Spread the smaller stones among the larger rocks with a spoon.

Use the spoon to spread dirt over streambed. Use dark-color dirt where the water is to appear deepest.

Spray the area with "wet" water, then matte medium.

Pin the clear styrene to the streambed and apply epoxy to secure it.

Apply a thin layer of clear caulk to the styrene with a small brush.

Apply Lexel clear sealant over the rock faces to represent cascading water.

Use a brush to dab a small amount of white latex caulk to the base of each falls. The white will show through the clear, giving the appearance of churning water.

Brush a coat of acrylic gloss medium onto the falls. Keep the brush moving vertically. You can apply multiple coats of gloss medium, but let each coat dry thoroughly.

Swirl acrylic gloss medium onto the flat surfaces of the water. The medium will go on white but dry clear and glossy.

Work the ground cover and trees up to the edge of the stream, then use a stiff-bristle brush and long vertical strokes to apply a thin layer of latex caulk to the surface of the .010" plastic waterfall, **11**. This will give the illusion that water is pouring over the dam and onto the stream bed below.

Apply a generous amount of clear caulk at the base of the falls to represent the turbulence that would occur there. Be sure to use latex caulk, as silicone-based caulk can craze or attack the styrene. Apply beads of Lexel (a clear caulk/sealant) along the tops and over the rock faces to represent the water cascading over them. The Lexel also provides a dam for the Enviro-Tex that will be poured later, **12**.

Once the clear latex caulk and Lexel dry, dab small amounts of white latex caulk at the base of the falls to represent the foam created by the turbulence of the water, **13**. Latex caulk dries to a flat finish, so brush acrylic gloss medium over the caulk on the waterfalls to give it a wet look, **14**.

After everything has dried for a day or two, mix and pour Enviro-Tex into the riverbed. Enviro-Tex dries very smooth and level, making it great for still water, but for a running river, we need to add some waves. To do this, apply a coat of acrylic gloss medium on top of the Enviro-Tex with a stiff-bristle brush. Work slowly to minimize air bubbles, and swirl the brush in a fan-like motion to create the impression of fast-flowing water, **15**. The gloss medium goes on milky white, but dries glossy and clear. You can also use thin coats of gloss medium to freshen up any older water scenes where the water has become scratched or dinged.

CHAPTER THIRTEEN

Stone walls and barbed wire

A combination of stone walls and a barbed-wire fence keeps the cows in the barnyard and off the tracks in this HO scale scene.

Stone walls are common in the Northeast and other areas. As farmers cleared stones from fields, they piled them along the perimeter of each cultivated or grazed area. This cleared the fields and helping mark farm boundaries. With the introduction of barbed wire, farmers added wire fences along their stone walls to keep cattle in place.

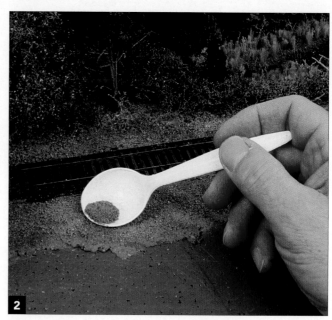

I collected a can of stones and gravel from a rural road. Run the stones for your wall through a kitchen sieve. Save the finer material for other scenery uses.

Sprinkle on dirt and foam as with the other scenicked areas on the layout.

I found the raw material for my walls along the side of a local dirt road. I just scraped up a bit of the stuff and ran it through a kitchen sieve until I was left with scale-size wall stones. I also found my fenceposts on field trips. They are actually sections of small twigs broken from brush growing along the roadside.

Just as the farmers did, I turned to a commercial supplier for my barbed wire. It is produced in sizes that will work with both HO and O scales by Scale Link Company of Great Britain (see page 94).

Use a kitchen sieve or screen wire to separate the wall stones from the unwanted dirt and gravel, **1**. Decide where you want to locate your wall, then begin by spreading out a thin layer of "ground goop" (see Chapter 3). Next, sprinkle on assorted textures of real dirt and ground foam, **2**. Using pump sprayers, apply "wet" water followed by diluted matte medium, **3**.

Trim off the top of the fencepost (twig) 4 scale feet above a set of buds, **4**. Trim off the base of the post 2 scale feet below the set of buds, **5**. To prepare for installation, use a scale rule to measure the distance between posts (approximately 8½ scale feet) and use a foam nail to punch a hole in the scenery base, **6**. After dipping the base of the fencepost in Weld Bond glue, install it using tweezers, **7**.

Build the wall stone by stone. Dip a stone in Weld Bond glue and place it in position (larger specimens at the bottom) with tweezers, **8**. Apply a generous coating of diluted matte medium to fix everything in place, **9**.

Use a foam nail to apply a dab of five-minute epoxy or thick super glue to the fenceposts (two posts at a time), **10**. Press the barbed wire into place with your fingers or tweezers, **11**. After the glue dries, paint the wire with brown model paint to simulate rust.

To flatten the finish of the stone wall, brush the stones with various shades of gray chalk, **12**. You can, of course, make standard barbed-wire fences without the rock walls as well.

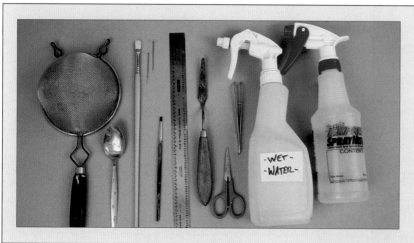

Tools:
- Kitchen sieve
- Artist's spatula
- Pump sprayers
- Small scissors
- Scale rule
- Foam Nail (or large pin)
- Tweezers
- Small soft-bristle paintbrush for model paint
- Small stiff (oil-type) paintbrush for dry pigments

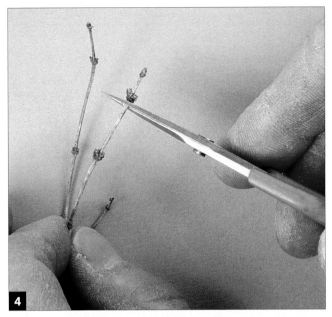

3 Fix the ground materials with a spray of "wet water" followed by a coat of diluted matte medium.

4 I used small twigs as raw material for my fenceposts. Start by trimming the top of each fencepost a scale 4 feet above a set of buds.

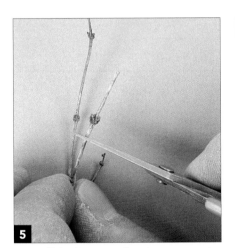

5 Trim off the bottom of each post a scale 2 feet below the buds.

6 Punch holes in the ground along the fenceline every 8½ scale feet.

Materials:

- Stones
- Sticks (fenceposts)
- Scale Link Company barbed wire:
  For HO scale use SL32F01,
  for O scale use SLOF30
- Weld Bond glue
- Five-minute epoxy
- Ground Goop mix: 1 cup
  Vermiculite, 1 cup Celluclay, 1 cup
  earth-color latex paint (Pittsburgh

  Tobacco Brown), ⅓ cup white glue,
  1 capful of concentrated liquid
  Lysol, and water
- Assortment of dirt and ground
  foam
- "Wet water"
- Brown model paint
- Matte medium
- Weber/Costello Alpha Color Hi-Fi
  Grays (dry chalks)

Dip the base of a post in Weld Bond, then use tweezers to install it in its mounting hole.

Build the wall by dipping each rock in glue and setting it in place.

Apply diluted matte medium over the entire stone wall to make sure all of the rocks stay in place.

Apply a small dab of epoxy or super glue to the top of each post.

Cut the brass barbed wire from its fret and press the wire into place on the epoxy on each post.

To blend the finish of the stones, use a brush to apply various shades of gray chalk.

CHAPTER FOURTEEN

Making a farm field

It's getting late in the day as Farmer Cobb takes a break from plowing to watch Rutland no. 403 roll past his field. This scene is in HO scale, but the techniques here can be applied to other scales as well.

Considering this country's agricultural history, logic would dictate that a tilled farm field should be a part of almost any American-prototype model railroad. Farms can be found in almost every region, and whether you model the steam era or today, a tractor working a field makes for a distinctive scene.

1 The HO plowing template is a piece of sheet styrene with one end cut with pinking shears.	**2** Spread a thin layer of ground goop mixture over the scenery base, covering the farm field area.
3 Lightly mist the ground goop with "wet water" to make it easier to work texture into the material.	**4** Slowly pull the styrene plow template through the goop to make furrows.

Before explaining how I created the tilled field in this project, I turned for advice to my friend Rich Cobb, who spent his childhood living and working on a farm in upstate New York. By providing an understanding of the basic steps necessary to prepare a field for planting and harvesting, he helped me better understand the effect I wanted to create. Here's Rich:

A lesson in farming
by Rich Cobb

Up until the late 1960s, the accepted practice in farming was to plow the land prior to planting a crop. This not only turned the grass and weeds under, but also mixed in any manure that might have been spread on the field. Flat fields were usually plowed in the longest dimension of the field,

Tools:
- Artist's spatula
- Pump sprayers
- Spoon
- Tweezers
- Kitchen sieves
- Plastic tilling template

5 Use a spoon to sprinkle finely sifted real dirt across the still-wet surface of the field.

6 Vacuum up any excess dirt to make sure the furrows are still visible. Don't touch the vacuum to the surface.

with furrows perpendicular at the ends. Hillsides were plowed across the hill to minimize erosion. Plowing left furrows in the field about 12" apart and large clumps of soil.

The next step was to use a disc harrow. This was a series of sharp wheels (discs) that broke up the lumps and smoothed out the field (Woodland Scenics makes an HO tractor/disc harrow set, no. 207). An alternative was a spiked-tooth harrow, which was a frame with rows of spikes that broke up the lumps. This was sometimes used after discing if a particularly level surface was desired, such as for a hay field.

Farmers in the Northeast planted a variety of grasses: hay, alfalfa, clover, timothy, orchard grass, and others. Crops included corn, oats, wheat, and in recent years, soybeans.

Corn was planted with a corn planter. In early years a two-row planter was used that required an operator on it. Rows were planted about 30 inches apart so that the tractor and cultivator could be used for weed control. In the 1960s and '70s the development of selective herbicides made the use of cultivators unnecessary. A corn planter consisted of a wedge-type shoe for each row that opened the soil. A container above the shoe fed in small amounts of fertilizer, and a second container held the corn seed, which was selected by a notched wheel that dropped a seed about every two inches. Behind the shoe was a flat wheel that packed the soil down on top of the seed and fertilizer (Woodland

Scenics has a tractor/planter set, no. 208).

Oats and wheat were planted with a grain drill—a large rectangular box with wheels at either end and shoes spaced every couple inches apart, which opened the soil for the seed.

Hay was planted with a seeder—a hand-cranked mechanism with a small canvas bag for seed that was hung over the shoulder as a farmer walked up and down the field. Later years saw the development of tractor-pulled seeders. Following planting, the field was usually gone over with a roller to press the seed into the ground.

Hay would probably be harvested for several years from a field. The field

Materials:

- Ground goop mix: 1 cup Vermiculite, 1 cup Celluclay, 1 cup earth-color latex paint, ⅓ cup white glue, 1 capful of concentrated liquid Lysol, and water.
- Fine sifted dark dirt
- Scenic Express Farm Pasture Blend Flock and Turf, with business-card magnet applied to bottle cap
- Matte medium
- "Wet" water (water with a drop or two of liquid dishwashing detergent added)
- Masking tape

7

Mist the field with matte medium to secure the dirt.

8

Press the tractor into the damp ground goop.

9

Use tweezers to simulate the depressions made by the plow.

10

Test fit the plow and tractor.

11

Cut the magnet from the backing.

would then be used for a pasture or plowed under for a grain crop. The same would be true for grain crops. After several years a different crop would be planted.

Harvesting

Hay was cut with a mower and then allowed to dry several days before being raked into windrows with a hay rake. In early days the hay would be pitched into wagons with pitchforks. Later a mechanical hay loader was developed that was pulled behind the wagon. The farmer would stand on the wagon and stack the hay as it came off the loader. The 1940s saw the development of tractor-drawn hay balers. Early ones

had four-cylinder air-cooled Wisconsin motors. Later models were powered by a power-take-off shaft from the tractor.

Bales were either rectangular in shape, tied with twine or wire, or round. The round ones withstood rain better, as only the outer layer would spoil, but the process was a lot slower. In either case, the farmer tried to get the hay into the barn before it got wet. In early years the bales were dropped on the ground and loaded by hand onto the wagon. Later years saw the development of chutes to carry the hay from the back of the baler to the wagon. This still required a worker to stack the bales on the wagon, or "kickers"—mechanisms that threw the bales into a

wagon with sides and a back on it.

At the barn, loose hay on the wagon was picked up by a hay fork, which pulled the hay up to the peak of the barn. There it moved on a track to the desired mow, where it was dropped. Bales were unloaded by hand, or else an elevator carried the bales at an angle up into the mow, where someone stacked them.

Corn in the early years was also cut by hand, stacked on a wagon, and taken to the silo, where a stationary blower chopped up the corn and blew it up a pipe into the top of the silo. The next development was a harvester that cut one or two rows of corn at a time and tied the stalks in bundles, which still had to be moved by hand to the silo. In the 1940s corn choppers were developed. Either self-propelled or run by a tractor, the chopper cut up the corn in the field and blew it into a wagon, which was then unloaded into the blower at the silo. The wagons had movable chains on the floor or movable gates that moved the corn into the blower. The 1940s also saw the development of the corn picker—a tractor-powered device that picked the ears off the corn stalks and loaded them in a wagon for feed grain. Later the combine was developed, which removed the ears from the stalks and then removed the individual kernels of corn from the cobs.

Grains were harvested with threshing machines—originally large machinery that was parked near the barn. The wheat or oats were brought to

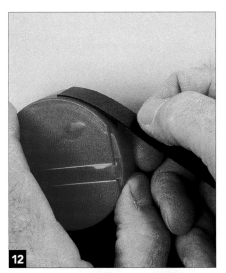

12

Apply the magnet strip to the Scenic Express bottle cap.

13

Once the field is dry, mask all areas where you don't want flocking.

14

Mist the exposed ground with matte medium.

it from the field. Later, tractor-powered machines were made that could go into the field. Still later, combines took over the job. The straw from either crop was usually baled up to be used as bedding for the livestock.

Modeling

Since I had recently become the proud owner of an HO scale GHQ 1953 International Harvester tractor and "Little Gem" 3-bottom (blade) plow, I decided to create a field with the plowing in progress. Before I could do so, I had to come up with a tool that would replicate the look of plowed soil. Scrounging through my desk, I found a pair of pinking shears. I noticed that the distance between the points on the blade was a little over a scale 12". This very closely matched the distance between the blades of my Little Gem. I cut a piece of .020" sheet styrene about 1" wide and 2" long, then cut one end off with the pinking shears. This would be my plowing template, **1**.

Start by using an artist's spatula to spread an ⅛"-thick layer of ground goop (see Chapter 3) over the scenery base, **2**. Give the surface of the goop a light misting of wet water to make it more workable, **3**. Lightly pull the styrene template across the surface of the goop to create the furrows made by the plow, **4**. After making the furrows, use a teaspoon to sprinkle fine dirt over the surface of the Goop, **5**. Vacuum up any excess dirt so it does not fill in the

15

Apply Scenic Express flocking to the exposed surface of the field.

ruts in the goop, **6**. Use a pump sprayer to lightly apply a mist of diluted matte medium (1 part medium to 5 parts water) to seal the dirt in place, **7**.

Once you decide where you want to locate the tractor and plow, press-fit the tractor into the ground goop, **8**. The plow is very fragile, so use a pair of tweezers to make depressions in the goop that simulate the grooves made by plow blades, **9**. Test-fit the plow into the grooves, **10**, but remove all the equipment while the scenery dries.

While waiting for the field to dry, you can prepare to apply static-charged Scenic Express flock. This material stands upright on the surface. First use scissors to cut a strip of flexible magnet

material, **11**. I used business card magnetic backing pads I purchased from a local shipping store. These measured 2" x 3½" and ⅛₂" thick and have a self-stick backing on one side. Peel away the paper backing from the magnet. Stick the magnet to the side of the bottle cap, **12**.

When the goop and dirt are dry, use masking tape to cover the area of the field you don't want textured with grass, **13**. Use a pump sprayer to mist the exposed ground with matte medium, **14**. While the ground is still wet, shake the container of Flock & Turf texture over the prepared area, **15**. Don't reinstall the farm equipment until everything dries thoroughly.

CHAPTER FIFTEEN

Building a dirt road

Work goes on in Jebediah's wheel Repair Shop as Rich Cobb and Art Fahie, two local boys, exchange some gossip. The dirt road in this On30 scene shows some wheel ruts from passing cars and wagons. The large building in the background is the Staton Inn.

There was a time when almost all the roadways of this country were dirt. Before widespread use of automobiles and trucks, railroads and trolleys provided the most efficient means of transportation. Paved (or even gravel or oiled) rural roads were not a high priority. City streets were often paved with bricks, stones, or gravel, but these improvements usually ended at the city limits.

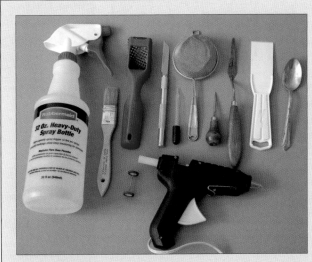

Tools:

- Spray bottle
- Brush
- Rasp
- Foam knife
- Eye dropper
- Screen
- Punch
- Spatula
- Putty knife
- Hot glue gun
- Wheel set

Materials:

- Latex paint
- Fine and coarse dirt
- Diluted white glue
- Foam Putty
- Ground goop
- Fine leaf foliage
- Leaves
- White glue
- Foam sheets

By the mid-1900s, most dirt roads had been upgraded to hard pavement or at least gravel (see Chapter 16). However, if one travels far enough off the interstates and highways of 21st-century America, it is still possible to find a few dirt roads, especially among farm fields in the rural areas of the Midwest and West.

Creating a miniature dirt road is not difficult, and by utilizing the inherent qualities of my "ground goop" mixture (see Chapter 3 for details), I found that it was possible to enhance the appearance of them. Let me explain.

When autos or trucks roll along a dirt road, especially during or following a rainstorm, they inevitably create ruts—sometimes deep ones—along the length of the road surface. When the base for a modeled dirt road is made

from ground goop it's easy to replicate this feature. The following steps are on my On30 Sandy River & Rangeley Lakes layout, but the same techniques will work in other scales as well.

Roadway base

Before we get around to making the surface of our road we must first establish a base for it. I've always been a firm believer that, when creating a scene, even the smallest elevation changes make that scene more visually interesting. This also applies to roadways. Since my On30 Sandy River railroad is built on a base of laminated 2"-thick foam sheets, it would have been easy to forget this fact and build my miniature roadways directly on that flat surface. In doing so, however, the roads would be particularly uninterest-

ing. It's much better to make them undulate a bit.

Doing this is easier than you think when working with foam. Let's look at the road running past the Staton Inn as an example. The road from Strong to Kingfield runs in front of the building, parallel to the SR&RL tracks. The Inn sits on a low hill, actually a sheet of Woodland Scenics ½" foam.

To make a road surface that undulates, I started by cutting random lengths of ¼" Styrofoam a scale 16 feet wide (the width of the road) with a Foam Knife, **1**, and hot gluing them to the surface of the 2" base foam at irregular intervals, **2**. I beveled the edges of the foam with a rasp, filled any voids with Woodland Scenics Foam Putty, **3**, and let the putty dry. When I was happy with the final surface, I

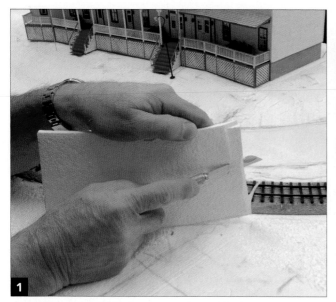

Cut the ⅛"-thick foam sheets into the width of the road, then cut them to random lengths.

Glue the road base pieces to the layout surface.

Bevel the edges of the foam road pieces with a rasp and apply Foam Putty to any gaps.

Apply ground goop to to the roadway and surrounding areas.

painted the surface of the foam with earth-color latex paint in preparation for the application of ground goop.

I used a spatula to apply a ⅛"-thick layer of goop to the road and neighboring areas, working in about a three-square-foot area at a time, **4**. I sprinkled the entire area, including the road surface, with fine sifted dirt, **5**.

Next, to delineate the roadway from the ground on either side of it, I spread coarse dirt along both sides of the road, **6**. This represents the larger particles of dirt and small stones and rocks that would accumulate there.

Here's where the final texture and detailing comes in. I found a set of HO scale tractor tires, remounted them on an axle extended to O scale, and rolled it along the road to create ruts in the still-wet goop, **7**. You can obviously use wheels from a vehicle in any scale that you model.

After applying additional coarse dirt and leaves to the roadsides and ground beside the road, I sprayed the entire area with "wet water" (tap water with a couple drops of liquid dish detergent added) and followed up with an application of diluted white glue

(1 part glue to 2 parts water) in an eyedropper, **8**.

As you go through this process you might notice areas where the paint in the goop bleeds through the dirt. Just reapply dirt, water, and glue as needed until the goop is completely covered, **9**.

Finally, I added various colors of Woodland Scenics fine leaf foliage to represent shrubs and weeds and Scenic Express "grass clumps" to add more texture and color along the road. Don't be concerned if everything looks wet and messy at this stage. In a few hours it will be completely dry, **10**.

5

Apply finely sifted dirt over the ground goop.

6

Use a spoon to apply coarse dirt and pebbles along the edge of the roadway.

7

Roll a pair of wheels along the still-wet ground goop to form ruts.

8

Apply diluted white glue along the road to secure the dirt and rocks.

9

Reapply dirt of different textures to any areas where the ground goop shows through.

10

The finished road looks like dirt—because it *is* dirt.

CHAPTER SIXTEEN

Gravel roads

Rutland RS-1 no. 403 crosses Maple Street as it heads south on the Rutland, Vt. to Chatham, N.Y., branch.

Since the 1950s, most major roads and highways in the country have been paved with macadam or concrete. However, many lesser-used rural roads, maintained by counties and townships, remain unpaved. For that reason, it is still possible to find town and county roads that are either unpaved, covered with gravel or crushed rock, or that have been paved and later coated with tar and a layer of gravel. I decided to replicate that type of roadway on my HO layout.

Tools List:

- Artist's spatula
- Teaspoon
- Fine kitchen sieve
- Scale Scenics Micro Mesh brass screen
- Pump sprayers

Materials:

- Ground goop mix (see Chapter 3)
- Stone dust, available at well-stocked stone and gravel or landscaping companies
- Matte medium, diluted 1 part medium to 5 parts water
- Highball Products N scale fine dark gray ballast
- "Wet" water (tap water with a few drops of dishwashing liquid added)
- Ground-up leaves (see Chapter 7)
- Assorted textures of dirt
- Assorted textures of ground foam
- Scenic Express summer lawn blend flocking

While rummaging through my supply of scenery materials, I found a bag of Highball Products N scale dark gray ballast. This material is fine enough to do a good job of representing gravel in HO or O scale, and will look good when applied. However, a home-improvement project led to a discovery of another new (to me) material that I like even better.

About the same time I was starting this project, I hired a local mason to install a brick walkway to my front porch. Instead of mortar, he was using a product called stone dust to fill the gaps between the bricks. After taking a closer look at the stone dust, I decided to use it, in combination with the ballast, to create a gravel or crushed-stone road. Stone dust is available from landscaping companies in a variety

of colors, which is helpful if you're matching colors unique to a certain region. You can also blend colors to represent the varied look of some gravel.

Build the road subgrade so that the road surface is taller than the

surrounding scenery. Use thin foam sheets as shown with the dirt road in Chapter 15. Gravel roads generally have a more even profile than dirt roads.

As with the dirt road, use a spatula to spread a thin layer of ground goop

Spread ground goop onto the road base.

Use a sieve to sprinkle ballast on the road surface.

Work the surrounding scenery up to the edge of road. A spoon allows a lot of control when adding dirt, ground leaves, and ground foam.

Once everything is in place, use a pump sprayer to mist "wet water" onto the road surface and adjacent scenery materials.

(see Chapter 3) onto the road base and surrounding area, **1**.

While the goop is still wet, use a fine kitchen sieve to sprinkle the ballast over the goop on the road surface, **2**. After thoroughly covering the goop with

gravel, work the surrounding scenery materials (ground foam, dried leaves, and dirt) up to the edge of the road, **3**.

Once all the scenery materials are in place, use a pump sprayer to soak everything with "wet water" (water

with a few drops of dish detergent added), **4**. Next, use a pump sprayer to apply a generous amount of diluted matte medium (1 part medium to 5 parts water), **5**. Use a spoon to fill any irregularities or low spots in the

5

Fix the scenery materials with matte medium.

6

Add more ballast if any bare spots develop.

7

Apply the stone dust through a piece of fine brass mesh.

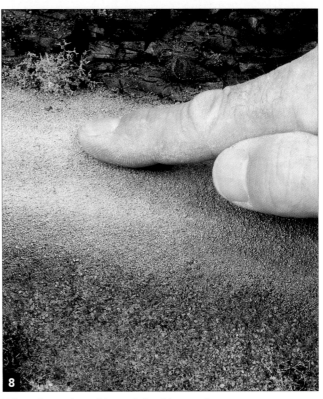

8

When the surface dries, rub it with your finger.

dampened road surface with additional ballast, **6**.

Now you can apply the stone dust. Start by filtering it with the same fine sieve you used to apply the ballast). Sift the dust onto the wet road surface by placing a spoonful of dust on a piece of very fine brass screening. Scrape a spoon across the stone dust, forcing it through the screen and onto the road surface, **7**.

Finally, after everything dries thoroughly, create a varied appearance by rubbing your finger along the road to smooth the surface of traffic lanes to simulate where the vehicle tires have pulverized the stone and softened the texture of the surface, **8**.

CHAPTER SEVENTEEN

Ready-mix concrete streets

While filling his Model A sedan at the local Texaco Station on Route 50 east of Kingfield, Ed Stiles' mouth begins watering when he sees Albert Rich's Model T Ford popcorn truck pull in. The realistic concrete roads add a lot to this O scale scene.

I have always had a fond recollection of the old concrete highways of the 1940s and '50s. Even today I can still recall, as a little kid sitting in the back seat of my father's Ford, hearing the thumping of the tires rolling over the expansion joints in the concrete while traveling the main roads around my family's home in upstate New York.

Because of a 1960s highway relocation, a four-mile stretch of old New York state Route 9 a few miles north of our home was still in existence in 1980. Since I wanted to replicate the concrete roads I remembered from my childhood on my 1940s era HO scale B&M West Hoosic Railroad, my wife, Cheryl, and I decided to visit that stretch of road to take some photos and measurements. Photo **1** was taken there in the early 1980s. It has since been repaved in blacktop.

Initially, I used styrene sheets to replicate my HO scale concrete roads but some years ago I switched to a product called Scalecrete. A few years ago the owner of Scalecrete Company called to tell me he was retiring and that Scalecrete would no longer be available. At the same time he revealed that he used a product called concrete patch, made by the DAP Corporation,

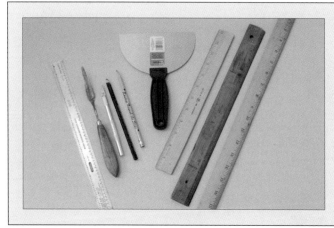

Tools:

- Scale rule
- Artist's spatula
- No. 11 hobby knife
- Foam pencil
- No. 2 pencil
- Putty knife
- Wood rulers

as the basis for Scalecrete. The product is available at Lowe's and other hardware and home-improvement stores. It is a fine-grained, concrete-based material that comes pre-mixed.

I built my O scale road on a sheet of 2"-thick foam. Although this is O scale, you can use exactly the same

materials and techniques in HO scale—just adjust the dimensions.

Begin by marking the edge of the scale 18-foot wide pavement with a foam pencil, **2**. Next, lay masking tape on either side of the proposed roadway eight strips thick to serve as forms. Mark each of the strips in pencil every

Here's the road to Lake Moreau in upstate New York circa 1980. It is typical of concrete roads from the 1940s onward.

Mark the edges of the road with a foam pencil.

Mark the masking-tape forms every scale 20 feet as a guide for the expansion joints to come.

Use an artist's spatula to work the concrete patch to the surface. Make sure the entire road is covered.

20 feet where you will eventually locate the expansion joints in the concrete perpendicular to the direction of travel, **3**.

Glob the patch on the roadway and spread it with an artist's spatula, **4**. Run a putty knife along the length of the roadway while resting it on the masking tape on either side, **5**.

While waiting for the concrete patch to set up, mark two wooden rulers at 3¾" and 8¼" with blue masking tape. After allowing the patch to dry for about 30 minutes, lay these rulers on the masking tape and across the road. Place the third ruler on top of them at the 6" mark, along which you will scribe expansion joints at the centerline with a no. 11 hobby knife, **6**.

Immediately scribe the expansion joints perpendicular to the road, **7**. After about an hour scribe along the masking tape on each edge of the road and peel the tape away, **8**. Next, scribe random cracks in some of the concrete panels, **9**, to replicate the cracks seen in the photo of the prototype road in **1**. By spreading the concrete patch thinly (approximately ⅟₁₆"), when it dries minor cracks will appear, adding to the realism, **10**.

After everything is dry, finish the scenery on each side of the road using dirt, ground foam, and static grass. For highway signs I used various sets from Blair Line.

Materials:

- DAP concrete patch
- Masking tape
- Painter's (blue) masking tape

5 Spread the concrete patch with a putty knife. The masking tape helps ensure an even roadway surface.

6 Use wood rulers as shown as a guide for scribing a longitudinal expansion joint with a hobby knife.

7 Scribe lateral expansion joints with the hobby knife, using the earlier marks on the masking tape (and a wood ruler) as a guide.

8 Scribe along the seam between the roadway and masking tape, then carefully peel away the tape.

9 Scribe random cracks in the roadway as desired. Add just a few of these if you're modeling a new highway, but add many more for an older highway that's been through a few changes of seasons.

10 Small cracks will naturally form in the concrete patch when it is spread in a thin coat. These cracks actually help enhance the road's appearance, making it more realistic.

CHAPTER EIGHTEEN

Utility poles and lines

Poles and overhead lines are everywhere in real life, and modeling them enhances the realism of a modeled scene. This On30 scene is on my Sandy River & Rangeley Lakes layout.

One detail that really adds visual interest to a period layout is the presence of line poles along a miniature railroad's right-of-way, along with telephone and power lines along roadways. Unfortunately, too many model railroaders leave these poles looking like shiny plastic sticks devoid of wire, detracting from the realism they are attempting to create.

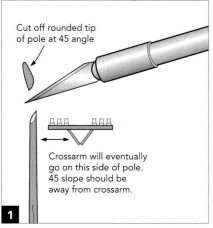

Cut off rounded tip of pole at 45 angle

Crossarm will eventually go on this side of pole. 45 slope should be away from crossarm.

1 Trim the tops of poles at 45 degree angle sloping away from crossarm.

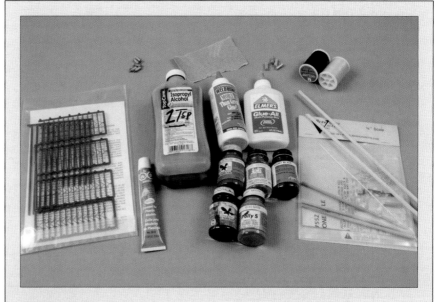

I found that, with Rix poles, button thread, and a little extra work, I could greatly improve the appearance of the telegraph, telephone, and power lines on my HO scale West Hoosic Division. I used many of the same techniques on my new On30 Sandy River & Rangeley Lakes.

In my area, 1950s railroad telegraph poles were from 15 to 25 feet tall. The number of crossarms per pole ranged from one to as many as five or six, depending on the location (main line or branch line). The busier the line, the more crossarms.

Utility poles on the other hand were usually about 30 to 35 feet high and carried both power and telephone services. The power lines, consisting of two or three wires, are the upper-most wires on the poles. To run the power to individual dwellings it must be stepped down from the primary lines' higher voltage to the secondary lines' lower voltage. Running it through a transformer takes care of this. The

Materials:

- HO Rix telegraph poles:
    30 and 40-foot poles
    72 crossarms
- HO Selley Finishing Touches (Bowser Mfg.):
    Line pole transformers
    Large transformers
- O scale Berkshire Valley Inc.:
    Telephone poles
    Transformers
    Electric meters
- Polly Scale (or other model paint):
    Earth
    Burlington Northern green
    Rail brown
    Roof brown
- Floquil Crystal Cote
- Testor's plastic cement
- Elmer's Glue-All (white glue)
- Weld Bond glue
- 3/16"-diameter basswood (for O scale power poles)

- Fine (100-grit) sandpaper
- India ink/rubbing alcohol mix: 1 teaspoon ink to 1 pint rubbing alcohol
- Light green no. 50-mercerized sewing thread
- Heavy black button thread

Tools (not shown):

- Alligator clips
- Foam nails (T-pins)
- Hobby knife
- Tweezers
- Razor saw
- File
- Assorted brushes
- Scissors
- Awl
- Rail nippers/wire cutters

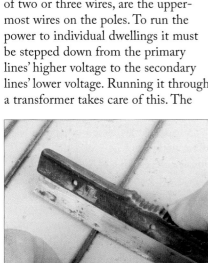

2 Pull a razor saw along the pole to create the effect of coarse grain.

3 Airbrush or brush-paint the pole with earth-color model paint.

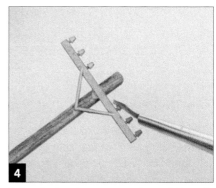

4 Paint the insulators green (I used Floquil Burlington Northern green).

Typical Rural Pole Line Detail

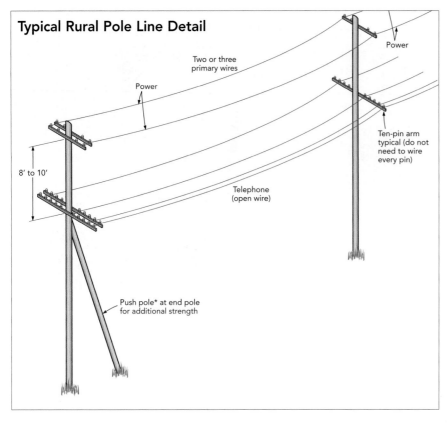

Two or three primary wires

Power

Power

8' to 10'

Ten-pin arm typical (do not need to wire every pin)

Telephone (open wire)

Push pole* at end pole for additional strength

Power Line Transformer Detail

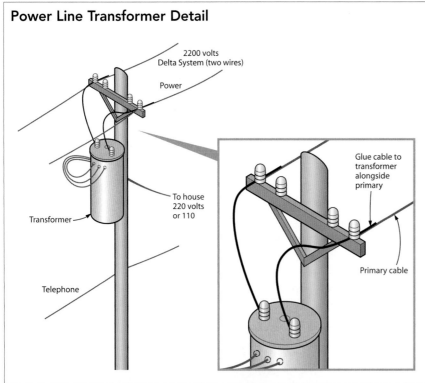

2200 volts Delta System (two wires)

Power

Transformer

To house 220 volts or 110

Telephone

Glue cable to transformer alongside primary

Primary cable

electric motors), three transformers were pole-mounted with the primary power run to each of the transformers. Service wires were then run to the building.

Telephone lines are strung a minimum of eight feet beneath the power lines. In urban areas, where the housing is dense, a telephone cable containing many individual wires is attached directly to each pole rather than using crossarms. The cable enters a terminal box where the wires are separated. One terminal box can handle up to 26 residences. Drop wires are run to each dwelling.

In a rural setting open, or individual, wires were the norm. These were strung on (up to) ten pin crossarms (As many as ten insulators can be mounted on each crossarm). As with electric lines, telephone wires are attached to the dwelling below the eaves of the house. The wire then runs down the outside and enters above the foundation. If the structure is brick or stone, the wires may have entered through a hole drilled in a window frame.

Guy wires or push poles are used at the end of runs or where one line intersects another. Crossarms are doubled on sharp corners or on end poles for additional strength. In the 1940s and '50s, pole insulators could be glass, ceramic, or even rubber. Glass insulators were either clear or various shades of green. Ceramic insulators were brown or white, and rubber insulators were flat black. Telegraph and telephone lines were usually uncoated copper. Since copper oxidizes and turns green with time, I used light green thread to replicate this. (There is an excellent article on line poles along with other helpful articles on lineside details in the Kalmbach book *Trackwork and Lineside Detail for Your Model Railroad*).

Poles and crossarms

Begin by removing the Rix poles from their sprues and cut them to the desired length. Trim their tops to a 45-degree angle with a hobby knife, **1**. Next, draw a razor saw along the length of the plastic pole to create

transformer is mounted to the pole below the power lines and above the telephone lines. The drawings above and on the facing page show this.

One transformer can serve several homes. The amount of power used by

each consumer is registered on a meter, which is attached to the side of the residence (or in its basement).

For mills, factories, and other businesses that used lots of electricity (typically with heavy-duty three-phase wood grain, **2**. Use 100-grit sandpaper to remove any excess plastic shavings.

After you've determined the number of insulators you want per pole, shorten the crossarms if necessary with a hobby knife. Apply a dab of plastic cement to the pole and place the crossarm and V-brace assembly into position.

When the glue has set, airbrush or brush-paint the entire pole assembly with Polly Scale earth (or similar) paint, **3**. Brush-paint the bottom of the pole Polly Scale roof brown to re-create the effect of age, weathering, and creosote treatment. Poles typically fade from dark to light from bottom to top as the creosote they are treated with wears away. Dip a brush in water and, working your way up the pole, blend the brown into the previously applied earth color. After the paint dries, apply a coating of India ink–alcohol to the entire pole.

If you don't have Rix's translucent green cross-arms, paint the insulators Burlington Northern green, **4**. For the green crossarms, paint the crossarms as you did the poles. When the paint dries, dab Floquil Crystal Clear onto each of the insulators to create a "glassy" appearance. Now paint the V braces flat brown.

To install the poles use a small awl to jab a hole in the Styrofoam scenery base. Dip the pole into Weld Bond glue and place it into the hole. For railroad line poles, position them 10 scale feet off the center of the track and 80 feet apart. Place power and telephone poles about 100 feet apart.

Stringing lines

For both HO and O scales I prefer heavy-duty black carpet/button thread for power cables and laterals to houses and industries. Dual-duty quilting thread works for telephone laterals from terminal boxes to houses. I use all-purpose light green sewing thread for open telephone wire. I've found the best representation of telephone cable to be Radio Shack acid-core solder (the thinnest variety available).

To add the wire, attach a spring clip to one end of the thread. Lay the thread over the first pole next to an insulator, **5**. Stretch the thread from

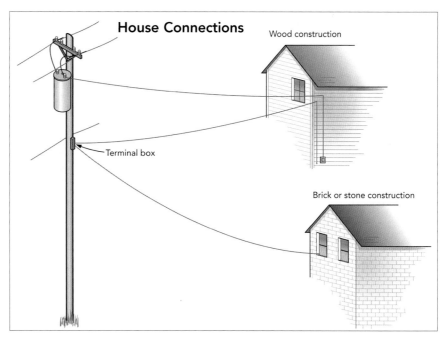

House Connections

Wood construction

Terminal box

Brick or stone construction

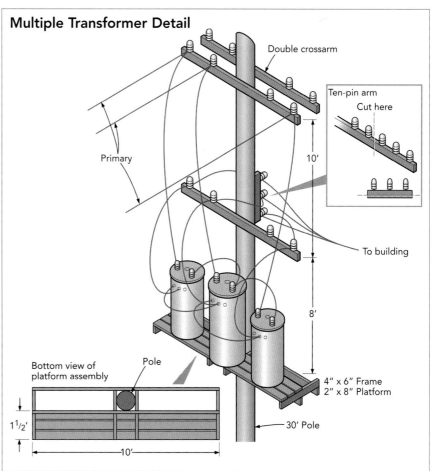

Multiple Transformer Detail

Double crossarm

Ten-pin arm

Cut here

Primary

10'

To building

8'

Bottom view of platform assembly

Pole

4" x 6" Frame
2" x 8" Platform

1½'

10'

30' Pole

pole to pole and attach another spring clip to the opposite end of the thread to keep the line taut, **6**. Use a pin to apply a small dab of white glue on each thread where it comes in contact with an insulator, **7**. (If a damaged line needs

to be repaired, you can dissolve white glue by applying a dab of water.) When the glue dries, trim excess thread from the crossarms with scissors.

To attach thread to the side of a building, apply full-strength white glue

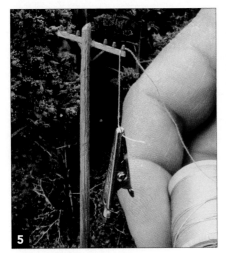

5

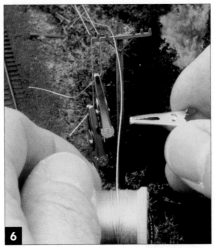

6

7

Attach a spring clip to the thread and lay the thread over the crossarm.

Attach a spring clip to the opposite end of the thread to keep it taut.

Apply a small dab of white glue to each insulator.

8

Multiple transformers serve the Peerless Tanning building.

9

Here's a typical urban power pole.

to the thread and press it in place. You can also run brass or metal wire down the side of a building. Be sure it's the same diameter as the thread and paint it black before gluing it in place.

For power lines I use Selley Finishing Touches line-pole transformers. Glue them to the pole with five-minute epoxy. For a multiple transformer assembly, **8**, I opted for one

Shelley large transformer flanked by two smaller ones. I attached the three wire secondary feed from the poles to an SS Limited industrial power head mounted on the side of the building. A single-transformer pole is shown in **9**.

Since I could not find a supplier of HO scale electrical meters for houses, I made my own from Plastruct strip styrene and transparent yellow rod,

10. Cut the strip to scale 12" lengths and the rod to scale 6" lengths. Paint the strip medium gray to represent the steel body of the meter box, then glue the rod to them to represent the glass meters.

For terminal boxes I used scale 12" sections of HO Central Valley rail fence gates I had laying in the bottom of my scrapbox. Photo **11** shows

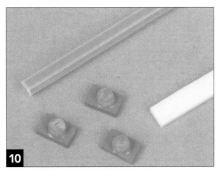

10

House electrical meters are made from Plastruct strip and rod styrene.

11

Terminal boxes were made from scraps of Central Valley fence gates.

how to trim them from fence gate to terminal boxes. Once they were cut to length I painted them silver.

In **12** we see a typical urban power pole. Note the push brace, the double crossarms (because it is the end of a run), and the transformer and terminal box with multiple laterals running to individual residences. The power and telephone cables are attached to the dwellings at the eaves and the wires run down the side of the house with the telephone line entering the just above the foundation and the meter box at the base of the power line.

I use the same techniques for building poles and lines in O scale that I do in HO, only this time I use poles, insulators, and transformers from Berkshire Valley Models instead of RIX. Berkshire Valley also carries electric meters, negating the need for scratchbuilding them as in HO. Berkshire Valley's poles and crossarms are basswood and the insulators are separate soft metal castings.

Since Berkshire Valley poles are meant for railroad rights-of-way, they are too short (24 scale feet) to be used as combination power/telephone poles. For this reason I substitute dowel (³⁄₁₆"-diameter basswood) for the main pole. After cutting it to 35-foot lengths

Typical Rural Pole Line Detail

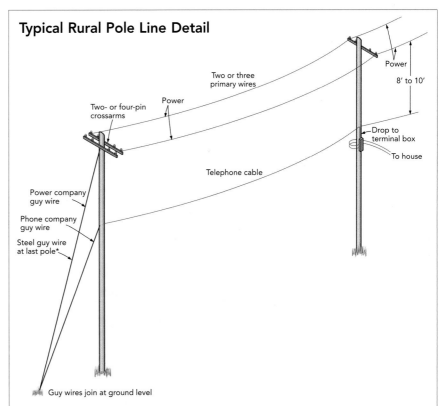

12

The power and telephone laterals are strung to the houses.

(2-3 feet will be buried in the foam base) and distressing the surface with a razor saw, add the crossarms and insulators, **13**, using Weld Bond cement. Paint the poles, crossarms, and insulators the same way as the Rix items and string them with the same thread as the HO lines. The house bracket seen in the photo on page 80 was made using a strip of basswood with three Berkshire Valley insulators glued to it.

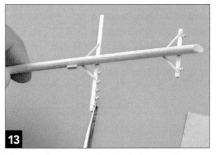

13

The insulators on the Berkshire Valley O scale models are separate pieces.

CHAPTER NINETEEN

Creating safe grade crossings

A Dandee Pretzel truck waits while Forney No. 9 crosses Adams Road on the On30 Sandy River & Rangeley Lakes.

In the 1930s and 1940s, the time period I chose to model, grade crossings were predominantly built using wooden planking. On my HO scale West Hoosic Division and O scale Sandy River Railroads I found the wood plank crossing protected by crossbucks relatively easy to build. I'm going to explain two methods I have used to do this: one for a dirt road and one for a blacktop crossing.

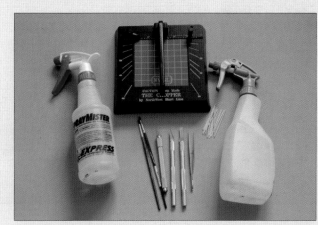

In either case, as you assemble the crossing, use a National Model Railroad Association standards gauge to be certain that the flanges of your equipment wheels will pass freely between the inside edges of the rails and the planking. Also, make sure that the height of the planks is a scale 2" to 3" below the rail height. Otherwise, the uncoupling pins on your locomotives and rolling stock could catch the ends of any offending planks.

To make a fully planked crossing, begin by using a small soft-bristle brush to spread ballast under the area you'll cover with planking, **1**. Apply "wet" water (water with a few drops of dish detergent added), then diluted matte medium with a pump sprayer.

Brush on a mix of India ink and alcohol (1 teaspoon ink to 1 pint rubbing alcohol) to stain the HO scale 4 x 8 stripwood planks.

Pull a razor saw along the length of each plank to distress the surface and create wood grain. Cut planks to the needed length with a razor blade or a NorthWest Short Line Chopper. Bevel the edge of planks that will be adjacent to the outside of the rail with a hobby knife, **2**. Glue the planks in position (directly to the ties of this Code 55 trackage), **3**. Use Duco cement, which is butyl acetate and acetone-based,

to avoid warping the thin pieces of basswood.

Depending upon the scale you model, code 83 or 100 rail may require thicker planking. Alternatively, you could also use wood shims on top of the existing ties, **4**.

Once the planks are in position, apply road material—dirt in this example—to the planks and secure it as with the ballast, **5**.

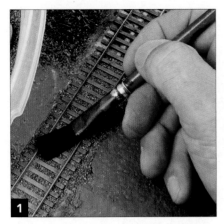

1 Spread ballast under the grade crossing area with a soft bristle brush. Make sure no ballast is on top of the ties.

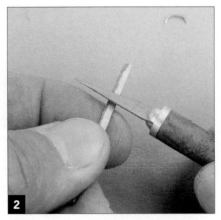

2 Bevel the edge of the planks that will be adjacent to the outside of the rail to clear the spike heads.

3 Apply Duco glue to the planks and press them firmly in place. Test-run a car to check the flangeway width.

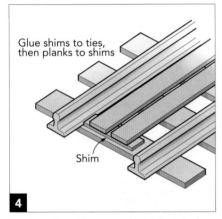

Glue shims to ties, then planks to shims

Shim

4 For heavier rail you can shim the planks up using thin stripwood or substitute thicker stripwood.

5 Use a spoon to spread the roadway dirt up to the grade crossing planking.

6 If you use Foam Putty or plaster as a road base, stain it with an India ink mix before adding the grade crossing.

7 When making a partially planked crossing for a paved road, add thin strips of masking tape over the planks and along the edge of road.

When building a partially planked crossing (planks next to the rails only), I prefer to fill the voids up to and between the ties with Woodland Scenics Foam Putty. Once the putty dries, stain it with a mix of two teaspoons India ink to a 7-ounce bottle of 90 percent rubbing alcohol, **6**. This keeps any white from showing through once the crossing is complete.

You can substitute styrene strip instead of stripwood to represent planks. I use the same procedure to prepare the strips for installation as

with the wood planks, only this time I paint them dark gray and glue them in place with liquid plastic cement.

Once the planks are in position, cover them with masking tape, **7**, and fill up to and between them with DAP concrete patch, **8**, my preferred material for blacktop and concrete roads (see Chapter 17). Let it dry for 15 minutes, then score the ready mix with a hobby knife, **9**, and remove the tape. Once the road surface has dried paint it grimy black to represent blacktop, **10**, or leave it natural to represent (you guessed it) concrete.

Now it's time to add Tichy Train Group crossbucks to protect the crossing. You can use the supplied posts or do as some prototype railroads did by making your own out of discarded rail. Use a no. 17 hobby knife blade to cut two pieces of code 55 rail to length. Apply five-minute epoxy to the

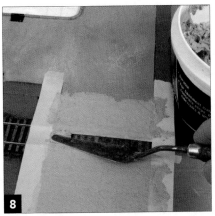

8

Apply the roadway material (DAP concrete patch for this crossing) between the planks.

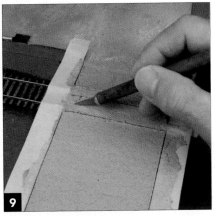

9

As when making highways, score the edges along the planks and peel the tape away.

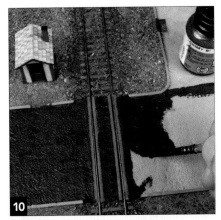

10

Paint hardtop roads the desired color. I used grimy black to simulate asphalt on this road and crossing.

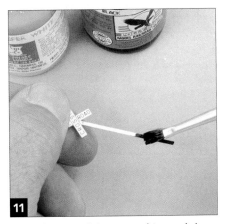

11

Paint the top of the post white and the bottom third black. This can vary based on era and prototype.

12

A small drop of Weld Bond glue will hold the post in place.

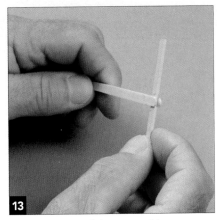

13

Notch the top of the post with a razor saw, then insert the cross-piece (sign board).

posts with a toothpick. Position the cross-buck on the post. Brush-paint the top of each post white to match the crossbucks and the bottom third black, **11**. Finally, apply a dab of Weld Bond to the bottom of the crossbuck assemblies and place them in position a scale 10 feet off the center line of the track, **12**.

In O scale I scratchbuild my crossbucks, using strip basswood and railroad crossing signs made on my printer, to match the real ones that were used on the prototype Sandy River & Rangeley Lakes. The main post stands about 17 feet high and is made from ⅛" x ³⁄₁₆" strip while the horizontal cross-member (sign board) is ¹⁄₁₆" x ³⁄₁₆" strip. (For HO scale, you can substitute ¹⁄₁₆" x ³⁄₃₂" strip with a cross-member of ¹⁄₃₂" x ³⁄₃₂" strip.)

Begin by notching the top of the main post with a razor saw. Insert the

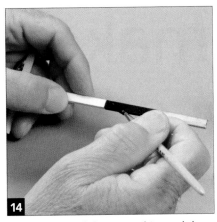

14

Paint the top of the post white and the base black.

10-foot-long long cross-member, **13**. Add a couple of Tichy Train Group nut-bolt-washer castings to the main post where the cross member is inserted. After painting the whole assembly white and the bottom of the main post black, **14**, print out a

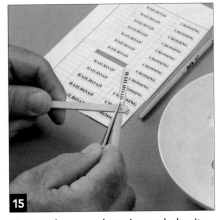

15

Cut out the paper lettering and glue it to the sign board.

batch of "RAILROAD CROSSING" lettering on your computer/printer the appropriate size and style to fit the sign. Glue the lettering in place with a thin coat of diluted white glue (Elmer's glue thinned with about 50 percent water), **15**.

CHAPTER TWENTY

Details make a difference

Lots of people are out and about at Spruce and Fulton streets as engine 403 slowly shoves a boxcar toward Peerless Tanning. This is an HO scene, but you can follow these guides to detail scenes in any scale.

No matter how well done your scenery is, adding small "real-world" details will always make it look better. Thirty-five years ago, when I first started construction of my HO scale West Hoosic Division, it was necessary to scratchbuild many of those smaller detail items. Since then, things had changed for the better, with many more detail items available for sale.

Check out a well-stocked hobby shop and you'll find a wealth of details. Tichy Train Group produces some very nice pre-painted styrene trackside details, including crossing signs, milepost markers, and whistle posts to use along the railroad right-of-way.

To detail roadways, I choose from Blair Line's vast assortment of .010" styrene highway signs, available in N through O scales. I've used the company's traffic signs, highway route markers, street signs, and vintage road signs.

Scale Structures Limited also has a number of items, including catch basins, manholes, and fire hydrants, that work well in a more urban setting.

While I was impressed with the Blair Line signs, I noticed that the only materials they supplied for posts were short lengths of either square basswood or round styrene rod. Both seemed rather heavy in cross section. I also felt it would be too repetitive to use only two types of posts for the various signs. I decided to substitute a variety of styrene shapes for posts, **1**. I opted for .030" round rod, .040" triangular strip, .030" square strip, and ³⁄₆₄" styrene angle.

I also decided to replicate the wooden guard posts often seen along highways in the 1950s. I used three different materials for this: ¹⁄₁₆" styrene rod, .060"-square styrene strip, and small lengths of twigs.

Sign preparation was simple. I painted the Tichy yellow railroad crossing signposts Polly Scale flat aluminum and the whistle signposts Polly Scale engine black. Since the mileposts had two sets of numbers on two separate faces and I could not find that style of post in any of my Northeastern railroad prototype photos, I scraped one set of numbers off with a hobby knife and installed the post with the remaining numbers facing the right side of the track, **2**.

The Blair Line signs are printed on a sheet of .010" styrene. After cutting out each sign with small sewing scissors, I used styrene cement to attach each sign to its post. I painted the backs of the signs aluminum and the posts various colors. After a

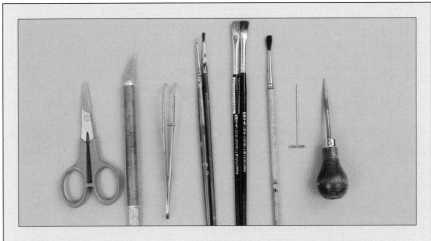

Tools List:

- Small sewing scissors
- Hobby knife with no. 11 blade
- Tweezers
- Small soft-bristle brushes, for painting posts
- Stiff-bristle oil-paint brushes, for applying pastels
- Medium-size soft-bristle brush, for applying India ink mix
- Woodland Scenics Foam Nail, for punching holes in scenery before installing smaller details
- Awl, for punching holes in scenery before installing larger details

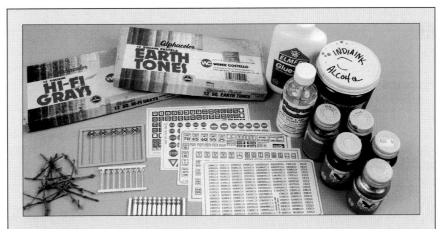

Materials:

- Twigs
- Evergreen Scale Models:
    ¹⁄₁₆"-diameter styrene
    .060"-square styrene
    .080"-square styrene
- Plastruct:
    .030"-styrene round rod
    .030"-styrene square rod
    .040"-triangle rod
- ³⁄₆₄"-styrene angle
- Tichy Train Group:
    Crossing signs
    Whistle posts
    Mileposts
- Blair Line:
    Highway signs
- Weber/Costello:
    Hi-Fi Gray pastels
    Earth-tone pastels
- Elmer's white glue
- Plastic solvent cement
- India ink–rubbing alcohol mix,
    1 teaspoon ink to 1 pint alcohol
- Polly Scale paints:
    Reefer Gray
    Flat Aluminum
    Roof Brown
    Engine Black
    Reading Green
- Scale Structures Limited:
    Manholes
    Catch basins
    Fire plugs, Call boxes

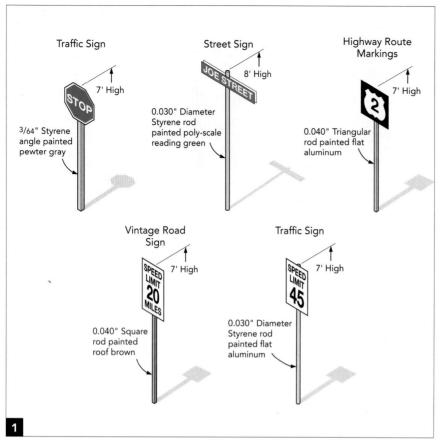

Traffic Sign
7' High
3/64" Styrene angle painted pewter gray

Street Sign
8' High
0.030" Diameter Styrene rod painted poly-scale reading green

Highway Route Markings
7' High
0.040" Triangular rod painted flat aluminum

Vintage Road Sign
7' High
SPEED LIMIT 20 MILES
0.040" Square rod painted roof brown

Traffic Sign
7' High
SPEED LIMIT 45
0.030" Diameter Styrene rod painted flat aluminum

1

For variety, I use various materials for the posts of my Blair Line signs.

light dusting of pastels, to soften the intensity of the colors, the signs were ready for installation.

Since I had four types of roads on my HO layout—blacktop, concrete, crushed stone, and dirt—I decided they would represent city, state, county, and town roads, respectively. I used 1/16"-diameter styrene rod to make

guardrails for the state roads and .060"-square styrene strip for square guardrails for the county roads. Both these are painted white and black. The round guardrails on my dirt town roads are simply small sections of twigs cut to length and left unpainted.

This same attention to detail works when creating a more urban setting. The

blacktop streets around Peerless Tanning Company, shown in the photo on page 90, has .080"-square styrene curbs, catch basins, manhole covers, fire plugs, and fire call boxes. I install the catch basins prior to applying the concrete-patch streets and the manhole covers after the patch has cured. I drill a 5/16" hole for the manhole cover in the road, then insert the manhole cover after applying some Weld Bond to it's bottom.

I also notch, paint, and install the curbs after the patch has dried. After notching them with a hobby knife every 5 scale feet, painting them gray, and applying some liquid plastic cement to the bottom of the curbing, it is pressed in place atop the outer edges of the asphalt. I bend the curbing for street intersections around a scrap piece of brass tubing while applying heat with a hair dryer.

Placing details

To get a better grasp of the impact these small details have on a scene, let's take a look at some photos. In the view on page 90, we are on Spruce Street looking west at the intersection with Fulton Street. From left to right we see a flanger lift flag in the distance, a mailbox, fire call box, street sign, speed limit sign, a Rix power pole with wires, crossbucks, an older (Preiser) gent carefully trimming the shrubs on the front lawn of the house on the corner, and a bathtub Madonna (a typical sight of the 1940s-50s).

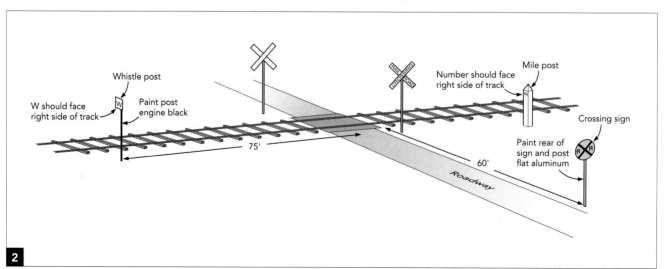

Whistle post
W should face right side of track
Paint post engine black
75'

Number should face right side of track

Mile post

Crossing sign
Paint rear of sign and post flat aluminum
Roadway
60'

2

This drawing shows the layout at a typical grade crossing. I modified Tichy mileposts as shown, so the number faces the right-hand side of the track.

Now we're on Spruce Street looking toward Fulton Street from the opposite direction of the photo on page 90.

We are looking northwest up Route 2 as a Rutland Alco diesel approaches Post Road grade crossing on its trip south from the railroad's namesake city.

Shifting to the left from the previous photo, we see the Rutland diesel at the grade crossing on Post Road.

This is the intersection of Maple Street and Route 2, looking southwest. Rutland RS-1 no. 403 is at the Maple Street grade crossing.

Study the street itself more closely. Notice the curbing with a catch basin just to the right of the fire call box and the manhole cover in the middle of the intersection.

In **3** we have walked back to Spruce Street and are now looking toward the intersection with Fulton from the opposite direction. From left to right are the fire call box, street sign, power pole, mailbox (painted as they were in the 40's in an olive drab color), cross-bucks, speed limit sign, the bathtub Madonna, a (Preiser) mother pushing her young'un down the sidewalk in a carriage, a fire hydrant and, finally, a yellow railroad crossing warning sign.

In **4** (out in the sticks) we have a U.S. route sign in the foreground while opposite it, on the left, is the back of a stop sign for the traffic on the dirt secondary road. Across the dirt road we have a street sign indicating that

this is, in fact, Post Road. Just to the left of the street sign, along the right-of-way, is a whistle post informing the engineer that he must sound the horn for the upcoming crossing. To the left of the whistle post, a cross-buck mounted on some old rail protects the grade crossing.

In **5** we have swung the camera to the left and can see, across the dirt road from the truck, the low-budget, unpainted guardrails the town has installed along with an old (vintage) speed limit sign. Note how the sign is more rusted and weathered in appearance than the route number sign in the first photo. This effect was created by brushing rust-colored dry pigments on the face of the sign.

In **6** we have the intersection of the crushed stone county road and the concrete highway. Note the better-maintained painted guard-posts along

the state road—the round ones in the left foreground—and the square posts just to the left of the locomotive along the county road. I created these by leaving the tops of the posts raw white plastic and painting the bottoms black. I then gave them a wash of India ink and alcohol to mute the colors.

In the middle foreground the street sign lets you know that this is Maple Street, while beyond the crossing there's a speed limit sign. On the far right, along the railroad right-of way, a concrete milepost indicates to the engineer that he is 41 miles from the beginning of this branch of the railroad.

These are just a few examples of how you can use details to enhance the realism of scenes across your model railroad. Check out the products available and use prototype photos and observation for more detailing ideas.

Suppliers and manufacturers

Activa Products
P. O. Box 1296
700 S. Garrett
Marshall, TX 75670
www.activa-products.com

Bar Mills Models
P. O. Box 609
Bar Mills, ME 04004
www.barmillsmodels.com

Berkshire Valley Inc.
P. O. Box 150
Adams, MA 01220
bvinc@berkshirevalleyinc.com

Blair Line
P. O. Box 1136
Carthage, MO 64836
www.blairline.com

**Tichy Train Group
(formerly Creative Model Associates)**
P. O. Box 220
Alamance, NC 27201-6220
tichytraingroup.com

Grandt Line Products
1040 B Shary Court
Concord, CA 94518
E-mail: Grandt@pacbell.net

GHQ
28100 Woodside Road
Shorewood, MN 55331
www.ghqmodels.com

Homabed
3568 Balls Ferry Rd.
Cottonwood, CA 96022
homabed.com

LARC Products
www.larcproducts.com

Micro Engineering
1120 Eagle Road
Fenton, MO 63026
www.microengineering.com

NJ International
P. O. Box 1029
Higley, AZ 85236
www.njinternational.com

Norton Company
(polishing pads)
www.nortonconsumer.com

**O&W Shops
(custom kit and scratchbuiding)**
109 Cayuga St.
Clyde, NY 14433
richinny@hotmail.com

Scale Link Company
Unit 27
Appins Farm Business Center
Farrington,
Dorset, UK, DT118RA
www.scalelink.co.uk

Scenic Express
175 Sheffield Drive #100
Delmont, PA 15626
www.scenicexpress.com

Selley Finishing Touches
Bowser Manufacturing
P. O. Box 322
Montoursville, PA 17754
www.bowser.trains.com

Tony's Train Xchange
Pinewood Plaza
57 River Rd., Suite 1023
Essex Jct., VT 05452
www.tonystrains.com

Woodland Scenics
P. O. Box 98
101 East Valley Drive
Linn Creek, MO 65052
www.woodlandscenics.com

Acknowledgments

I want to thank the following people and manufacturers for helping make this book possible:

Bill Brown (LARC Enterprises), Rich Cobb (O&W Shops), Art Fahie (Bar Mills Models), Bob and Ron Rands (Micro Engineering), Rick Rideout (Rix Products), Dale Rush (Blair Line), Jim Sacco (City Classics), Carol and Craig Freeland (Sterling Models), Martha Young (SS Limited), Loren Perry (Gold Medal Models), Richard Jayne (Homabed), and Kimber Stevens (Woodland Scenics).

Thanks also to the folks at Activa Products, Evergreen Hills Models, GHQ, Grandt Line Products, NuComp Miniatures, Jane's Trains, Selley Finishing Touches, Wm. K. Walthers, Scenic Express, and CS Designs.

A special thanks to my friends Scott Baroody, Dick Elwell, George Micklus, and John Nehrich. I can't leave out Kent Johnson and Jeff Wilson at Kalmbach Publishing Company.

As always, an extra-special thank you, with love, to my best friend and confidant—my wife, Cheryl.

—Lou Sassi

About the author

Lou Sassi has been interested in model trains since the late 1940s when his father gave him a Lionel train set for Christmas. His introduction to scale model railroading began when he discovered the December 1958 issue of *Model Railroader* magazine at a newsstand in his hometown of Saratoga Springs, New York.

After graduation in 1964 from the New York State Ranger School, a division of the College of Forestry in Syracuse, N. Y., Lou worked as a forest technician for the New York State Conservation Department. Two years later he accepted a position as a draftsman at General Electric's Large Steam Turbine Department in Schenectady, N. Y. After three years at a drafting table he moved on to the land surveying department of an engineering firm in Niskayuna, N. Y., where he was employed for 12 years. While there he obtained his professional land surveying license. He then worked 14 years for the Burnt Hills Ballston Lake School System, retiring in 2000.

Lou's cartoons, articles, and photos have appeared in many model railroad publications for over three decades. His former home layout, the Boston & Maine West Hoosic Division, was featured in the July 1988 issue of *Model Railroader* magazine, the 1996 and 1999 issues of *Great Model Railroads*, the Wm. K. Walthers product catalog, and Allen Keller's Great Model Railroads video series (no. 23).

Lou and his wife Cheryl have been married 47 years and have two grown sons, Adam and Aric. They also are the proud grandparents of two teenage grandchildren, Heather and Joshua Sassi.